C7-C0-CDU-058

ISSUES, STRATEGIES AND CONCERNS IN EDUCATION TODAY

ISSUES
STRATEGIES
AND
CONCERNS
IN
EDUCATION
TODAY

A collection of essays

Dr. Ralph G. Perrino

ISSUES, STRATEGIES AND CONCERNS
IN EDUCATION TODAY
Copyright © 2014 Ralph G. Perrino.
All rights reserved.

Publishing Consultant, Flying Pig Media
Cover & Interior Design by VMC Art & Design, LLC

The uploading, scanning, and distribution of this book in any form or by any means—including but not limited to electronic, mechanical, photocopying, recording, or otherwise—without the permission of the copyright holder is illegal and punishable by law. Please purchase only authorized editions of this work, and do not participate in or encourage electronic piracy of copyrighted materials. Your support of the author's rights is appreciated.

Second Edition, 2016

ISBN: 978-0-692-20576-1

To Denise, Without Whose Love and Support
This Book Would Not Have Happened

Table of Contents

Foreword

The field of education is replete with issues that seem complex, confusing and, at times, intractable to many parents and students. This is apparent at the elementary, middle, high school, and college levels. The result is that many parents and students often do not know where to find honest, factual information to guide them, or they make decisions without seeking authoritative sources of assistance.

This book serves as a guide for parents and students as they maneuver through the maze of issues, options, and decisions necessary for successful completion of the education experience from kindergarten through the college years. The process begins at birth when parents must (or should) consider the financial challenges associated with educating their children. It continues through the K-12 years where matters such as standardized testing, special education, gifted programs, course selection, and other critical subjects need to be addressed.

The decisions made during the K-12 years can, and often do, have significant consequences later in a child's academic career. Getting it right the first time can help pave the way to a successful elementary, middle, high school, and college experience.

The essays contained in this book are intended to do several things. Part 1, *Class, Culture, and the Education System,* examines the fundamental premise that there are forces often beyond our control that guide each of us through life. The socialization process is examined, as well as the "digital divide" between rich and poor in America that threatens to re-create a divided nation as described by Michael Harrington in *The Other America* more than 50 years ago.

There are also forces that we can control, but often do not, and that if managed effectively, can be used to our advantage. Issues such as inappropriate college selection predicated on peer, parental, teacher, guidance counselor, or other irrational sources of pressure are examined to help parents and students avoid heading off to college at the wrong age, at the wrong time, and for the wrong reasons. Also discussed in this section is the matter of "grit"—the latest term in academic circles to define what has traditionally been called persever-ance, determination, drive, and resilience in a student. This article, titled "Grit: The Missing Ingredient in the

Education of America's Youth," addresses the hidden factors at play that often determine the success of a student who faces obstacles.

Last, this section discusses the dramatic changes that have taken place in higher education just in the past decade, including distance learning, online degrees, and Massive Open Online Courses (MOOCs). On the one hand, these changes have begun to democratize higher education, but in the opinion of many scholars have the potential to create a two-tiered system of higher education in America—one for the wealthy and one for the poor and middle class.

Part 2 addresses *The Practical Side of Learning and Living*. Standardized examinations are discussed, and the basic questions asked are whether they measure the right skills to predict academic success in college, or are other, less quantifiable skills ignored in the rush to measure student achievement numerically? The essay "Bringing Drama to the Core: A Creative Approach to Teaching Core Subject Areas" asks whether non-core subjects like theater, art, and music can be used in the classroom to teach subject areas such as mathematics to students who simply require a different approach to learning. This section of the book also highlights the importance of "Matching College Degrees with the Job Market" and the critical role that the American community college system plays in our overall system of higher education.

Part 3, *"Understanding Financial and Program Options,"* takes a critical look at the SAT and ACT examinations, the often-controversial practice commonly known as the "early decision" college application process, the often-confusing college funding maze, and the issue of whether or not a student needs a tutor to help him or her succeed in school. These matters become critical as a student enters high school. Knowing the ins and outs of the SAT and ACT examinations can have a significant impact on a student's chances of attending college. Knowing the difference between early decision and early admission and whether it is in a student's best interest to pursue either course of action can contribute to a very important decision. Gaining an understanding of the college funding maze – the difference between a loan and a grant – not to mention the FAFSA application process, and the myriad of other financial considerations associated with funding a college education can be a daunting experience. Finally, knowing whether, how, when, and why to hire a tutor to help a student either succeed at a higher level or simply avoid failing is an issue that most parents are simply ill-equipped to address.

Part 4 is a philosophical as well as a practical look at the issue of entrepreneurship. Dr. Perrino has been a business owner for more than twenty years. During that time, he has experienced the difficulties of the business cycle and has weathered the worst economic downturn since the 1930s. His insights on the issue of business ownership provide the reader a framework for understanding both his business acumen and his unique sociological perspective on the world of business.

The most important thing to remember is that your child will be successful in spite of himself!

PART ONE

Class, Culture and the Education System

Is the Digital Divide an Impediment to Closing the Achievement Gap?

How the Digital Divide Affects Students

With an increased reliance on technology in and out of the classroom, the division between the digital haves and have-nots may result in a widening education gap in America. There also may be a potential link between the digital divide—the disparity in access to computers and the Internet between wealthy and poor—and the achievement gap between White/Asian and Black/Hispanic students in American public schools.

In a January 2013 article titled, "The Web-deprived Study at McDonald's," *Wall Street Journal* writer Anton Trolanovski stated that Internet access in the United States is influenced by family income and gave several examples. Tenth grader Dustin Williams from Cintronville, Alabama, travels to the McDonald's across the street from his high school to access the free Wi-Fi in order to do his homework. Joshua Edwards, another student from Cintronville, makes multiple trips to the same McDonald's to work on research papers. In Pinconning, Michigan, Jennifer LaBrenz, a single mom with a take-home income of $2,000 per month, drives her daughter to the local McDonald's to use the free Wi-Fi in the parking lot. She and her daughter sit in their car for hours while her daughter does her homework and sends emails to her teachers.

Sara Grossman, in a piece that appeared in the August 19, 2013, online edition of *The Chronicle of Higher Education* titled, "For Internet Access, Rural Students Have to Hit the Road," stated "19 million Americans lack access to high-speed Internet service, according to a 2012 report from the Federal Communications Commission (FCC)." She cited the growing gap between Internet access among rural and urban residents in the United States. The FCC reports in its findings that while only 1.8 percent of Americans in urban areas lack Internet access, 24 percent in rural areas cannot connect to the Internet. The link between lack of access to the Internet and the achievement gap between White/Asian students and Black/Hispanic students crystallizes in this environment. Further, this divide is evident in the urban/rural context.

Grossman offered yet another example. She reported that Dakota Bates, a student from Alton, Missouri, who attends Missouri State University, drives forty miles each way, four days each week to attend classes. In order to make use of the Internet, Dakota drives to the college to meet an 8:00 a.m. class, and stays on campus until late evening to complete his assignments. His home in Alton is five miles out of reach of an Internet connection. "The world wide web has turned into the world wide wait," in the words of Southeast Kentucky Community and Technical College Sociology Professor Roy Silver.

What Role Can or Should Government Play?

A U.S. Department of Commerce study in 1995 titled "Falling through the Net: A Survey of the 'Haves and Have Nots' in Rural America" examined the technology gap in American households. The result of this study revealed a wide gap between White and wealthy households and those with lower education levels. In 1998, the Clinton-Gore administration produced a report titled "Falling through the Net II: New Data on the Digital Divide." The following year, the administration convened a summit to address the emerging problem called the Digital Divide Summit. The result was several federal initiatives aimed at closing the gap between wealthy and poor families.

By 2004, a U.S. Department of Commerce study, "A Nation Online: Entering the Broadband Age," reported significant progress in closing the digital divide. This study stated that in 2003, 62 percent of homes had computers and 55 percent had access to the Internet. However, that same study showed that when these statistics are controlled for race, 65 percent of White households had Internet access while only 46 percent of Black households and 37 percent of Hispanic households did.

By 2010, recognizing the geographic and socio-economic disparities of broadband access across the nation, the Federal Communications Commission (FCC) launched *The National Broadband Plan*. The goal of this plan was to address the need to recognize broadband access as a critical element of the nation's infrastructure. This report pointed out that just as railroads during the 1860s, electricity in the 1930s, and the Interstate Highway System in the 1950s had united the nation and allowed it to innovate, prosper, remain secure, and serve as a global leader, broadband access in the 21st century would serve the same role.

The FCC's *National Broadband Plan* initiative recognized that broadband access alone will not "solve America's problems" nor will it guarantee that the United States will maintain its position of world leadership. It also cannot guarantee the best employment, education, health care, public safety and public services for all Americans. It can, however, in the view of the FCC, open the door of innovation and provide opportunity to those whose geographic location, income, and race limit access to the Internet.

Further indication that the federal government recognizes the urgency associated with this problem, the American Recovery and Reinvestment Act of 2009 included $250 million to reach out to Americans who do not have access to or have not yet adopted Internet technology (Congressional Budget Office, 2015).

If we are serious about ensuring equal access to information and opportunities between and among generations, this issue must be addressed.

The problem may be that the efforts of state, local, and federal government to level the playing field by bringing high speed Internet to students from poor families and rural areas may be too little too late to address the increasing separation of the haves and the have-nots in public education. Turtle Mountain Community College (TMCC), a tribal college located in rural North Dakota, is a case in point. The community surrounding TMCC is experiencing an unemployment rate of an astonishing 70 percent. Many students at TMCC simply have no access to the Internet. Those who do often use dial-up connections. The result is that many students are not skilled with the Internet search process and are hindered by lack of research skills. Getting assignments completed in this environment is sometimes a difficult task.

A 2006 study by Judy Salpeter in *Technology and Learning* reported that several high profile projects at the state level have been aimed at closing the digital divide, including Maine's Learning Technology program, Michigan's Freedom to Learn program, Broward County, Florida's Digital Learning Environment and an initiative launched in Jefferson County, Kentucky. Each of these efforts points to a growing concern about and awareness of the digital divide.

TMCC's president, James L. Davis, has said that many of the college's 1,325 students struggle just to get by and often cannot afford the cost of Internet service, let alone a computer. The U.S. Congress has approved $8,000 per student to help alleviate the problem, but so far has authorized only $6,000 per student. Davis emphasized that with more federal dollars, "We would be able to provide a better service in terms of academic education and training of our population. It would be a big key to reducing poverty and reducing unemployment."

Social Class Disparities and the Divide: Why Is It So Persistent?

Sarah Garland, in the August 18, 2013 issue of *The*

Atlantic, reports that this growing divide is not restricted to high school and college-age students. She points out that social class plays a major role in determining access to information. Garland observed and interviewed two families, one upper income White, the other lower income Black. What she discovered was interesting. When children are pre-school aged, upper income families are connected to play groups and other forms of social networks. It is there that they collect information. In this environment, Garland says: "Social class has become increasingly important in deciding outcomes for children." Simply stated, wealthy families have economic, social, and technological advantages that are not available to lower income families. Under these circumstances, the achievement gap may slowly simmer during the pre-school years and manifest itself with far more dramatic implications by the high school and college years.

A report by the NCES in 2001 titled "Computer and Internet Use by Children and Adolescents in 2001" revealed that among children and adolescents ages five through seventeen, 90 percent use computers and 59 percent use the Internet on a regular basis. Those percentages change depending on home or school use. According to the NCES report, 81 percent use computers at school and 65 percent use computers at home. In homes where parents had attained a graduate degree and those from families with incomes above $75,000, the school and home rate of computer use increased to 90 and 85 percent, respectively.

The digital divide emerges clearly at this point. When examined along racial/ethnic lines, the figures are significantly different. Forty-one percent of Black and Hispanic students and 54 percent of American Indian students use a computer at home, while 77 percent of White and Asian students use a computer at home. When family income is a factor, only 31 percent of students from families with an annual income of $20,000 use computers at home; 89 percent of students from families with incomes over $75,000 use a computer at home. The result, according to the NCES report, is that in 2001, White students were far more likely to complete school assignments using a computer than were Black and Hispanic students, by a margin of 52 to 28 percent.

In January 2004, the *Newsletter on Intellectual Freedom* reported, "While public schools have made huge improvements in providing computer and Internet access, minority and poor students lack computer access outside regular school hours."

In 2004, then Secretary of Education Ron Paige, stated: "The pace of technological change is truly astounding and has left no area of our lives untouched, including schools." Paige went on to say that although progress had been made, "…there are still big differences in home computer use that need to be addressed before we can declare the digital divide closed."

In 2013, the trend continued to show a strong correlation between family income and access to technology. Cecilia Kang of *The Washington Post* reported "a gap in access to the Internet between rich and poor is leading to disparities in education" (March 1, 2013). As shown in the aforementioned reports by NCES and the U.S. Census Bureau during the period 1998-2002, students are increasingly expected to use the Internet to complete assignments. The reality is that during the past fifteen years, that access has remained relatively stagnant. According to the *Post*, "Half of all students in higher-income families have access to the Internet at home." Conversely, 20 percent of middle-income students and only three percent of lower-income students have a home Internet connection. A study published in August 22, 2013 *Chicago Policy Review* confirms this data, stating that about one in four students in the United States do not have a computer at home, nor do they have regular access to the Internet (Raichert, 2013).

In a 2013 interview with Bill Moyers titled "Who's Widening America's Digital Divide," Susan Crawford, former special assistant to President Obama for Science, Technology, and Communications, pointed out that 19 million Americans simply have no access to the Internet, and 33 percent of the population do not subscribe because they simply cannot afford it. Crawford states: "We are creating, yet again, two Americas and deepening inequality through this communication inequality."

She observed that "parents around the country know that their kids can't get an adequate education without Internet access. You can't apply for a job these days without going online, you can't get access to government benefits adequately, you can't start a business. This feels to 300 million Americans like a utility—like something that's just essential for life." Moyers reports that 2013 data from the U.S. Department of Commerce indicates that four out of ten households with annual household incomes less than $25,000 reported having access to the Internet at home, compared to 93 percent of households with incomes greater than $100,000.

When asked by Moyers whether Internet companies are providing "cheap enough access to the poor folks in this country," Crawford said, "These are good American companies. Their profit motives, though, don't line up with our social needs to make sure that everybody gets access. They're not in the business of making sure that everybody has reasonably priced Internet access. That's how a utility functions. That's the way we need to treat this commodity. They're in the business, right now, of finding rich neighborhoods and harvesting—just making more and more money from the same number of people. They're doing really well at that…but they're not providing this deep social need of connection that every other country is taking seriously." She continues, "Having a communication system that knits the country together is not just about economic growth, it's about the social fabric of the country, and a country that feels as if it can move together and trust each other is one that is more democratic" (Moyers, 2013).

Questions and Possible Solutions

While it is true that there is a divide between rich and poor with regard to Internet access, can it be stated with certainty that one of the most significant factors impacting the growing gap in academic performance between rich and poor, urban and rural, and White/Asian and Black/Hispanic students is the digital divide? Maybe not.

The study by Salpeter in 2006 reported that although significant progress has been made in the attempt to provide computer and Internet access to a wider range of students, only 41 percent of respondents to her survey said that technology had helped raise standardized test scores, and that the achievement gap may not be affected as much as many would believe it has. Salpeter states: "With student achievement being measured these days almost exclusively through test results, it is understandable that there is ambivalence on the part of many districts about how much emphasis to place on student access (to technology)."

It is well established that there is a gap in access to computers and the Internet based on socioeconomic class. It is easy to assume that a strong correlation exists between access to technology and academic achievement. However, the question that needs to be asked is: Would providing computers to lower-income students at home address the issue of the achievement gap? The answer to this question may seem obvious on the surface; however, scientific research in this area is inconclusive. The study published in *Chicago Policy Review* reports that a 2013 paper by the National Bureau of Economic Research titled, "Experimental Evidence on the Effects of Home Computers on Academic Achievement Among Schoolchildren," written by Robert Fairlie and Jonathan Robinson, reveals some surprising results. Their study was the largest field experiment testing the hypothesis that providing free computers to schoolchildren would improve their academic performance.

Fairlie and Robinson surveyed 1,123 students in grades six through 10 in 15 California schools. Their findings revealed no significant correlation between provision of free computers to students and improved academic success. Not only did their research show no significant improved outcomes, it revealed a potential negative result. Variables such as improved grades, increased test scores, improved attendance, increased credits earned, or reduced disciplinary actions were not affected in a positive manner. Interestingly, Fairlie and Robinson did find that providing free home computers did increase the total amount of schoolwork completed by students, despite finding no significant increase in academic achievement. Oddly, they also found that provision of a home computer increased its use for entertainment purposes. Conversely, a study by Attewell and Battle in 1999 and others found positive impacts on academic achievement when computers were provided free to students for home use.

The lesson to be learned here is that there is value in searching, probing, making mistakes, even wasting time looking. It develops the "curiosity gene" and nurtures the mind. It also teaches self-discipline, doggedness, determination, resourcefulness, and resiliency. Students today seem to have few of those traits. Society may simply morph into a new form that accepts the digital age as the norm, but something valuable and irretrievable will be lost in the process.

There is no clear indication that a correlation exists between computer and Internet access and improved academic achievement. It is fair to say that, anecdotally, most people believe that a technologically savvy student has a better chance of academic success. However, before lunging into an endless spiral of costs associated with providing every student with a computer, a key issue needs to be addressed. Are we relying too much on technology to educate our children? It seems that everyone—superintendents of school districts, school board members, administrators, principals, and teachers—are falling over one another in a mad rush to digitize the learning environment. It is important to note that the basics will always apply. Not all learning must be digitized.

As a nation, we have somehow reached the point where we equate intelligence with technological savvy. Without a firm foundation in the basics—reading comprehension, math, writing, critical thinking skills, and problem-solving skills—technology will be of little help in closing the achievement gap. Is it not fair to state that a primary issue is weak family structure and poorly functioning urban public schools? Without a family unit that emphasizes the critical importance of academic achievement, spending public funds on technology is only a band aid approach to a broader problem. Without urban public schools that stress the basics of academic success—reading, math, writing, critical thinking, problem solving—technology is only a superficial tool with little, if any, long-term impact.

This may be summed up best by educational psychologist Jane Healy, who believes that there has been far too much attention given to closing the digital divide. Healy thinks other approaches to educational change may be more effective in closing the achievement gap. She has stated that wealthy parents may be disappointed to learn that all of the expensive technology in public schools may not be the ticket to success for their sons and daughters. Healy observes, "In wealthy schools where kids are becoming button-clicking, stimulus-seeking droids because they're on computers too much, the parents are going to be very disappointed with the outcome" and that a child with success in his or her future has "learned to think and to express himself well and to solve problems without a game attached" (Borsuk, 1999).

The issue of the achievement gap in our public schools is of major concern. Equally important is the digital divide between rich and poor. Both need to be addressed because they indicate inherent inequality in our schools and in society. However, the question remains: Are these two issues correlated, or do they stand on their own?

References

American Library Association (2004). "'Digital Divide' persists. *Newsletter on Intellectual Freedom 53.1,* 5. Retrieved from https://journals.ala.org/nif/issue/viewIssue/487/194

Attewell, P., & Battle, J. (1999, February). Home computers and school performance. *The Information Society, 15,* 1-10. doi: 10.1080/019722499128628

Borsuk, A. J. (1999, October 11). Struggle to close the "digital divide" has been a tough one. *The Milwaukee Journal Sentinel,* p. 8A. Retrieved from https://news.google.com/newspapers?nid=1683&dat=19991011&id=n3MaAAAAI-BAJ&sjid=Vi8EAAAAIBAJ&pg=6743,641726&hl=en

Congressional Budget Office. (2015). *Estimated impact of the American Recovery and Reinvestment Act on employment and economic output in 2014.* (CBO Publication No. 49958). Washington, DC. Retrieved from https://www.cbo.gov/sites/default/files/114th-congress-2015-2016/reports/49958-ARRA.pdf

Fairlie, R. W., & Robinson, J. (2013). Experimental evidence on the effects of home computers on academic achievement among school children (Working Paper No. 19060). *American Economic Journal: Applied Economics, 5*(3), 211-240. Retrieved from National Bureau of Economic Research website: http://www.nber.org/papers/w19060

Federal Communications Commission. (2010). *The omnibus*

broadband initiative: National broadband plan. Retrieved from https://transition.fcc.gov/national-broadband-plan/national-broadband-plan.pdf

Garland, S. (2013, August). When class became more important to a child's education than race. *The Atlantic.* Retrieved from http://www.theatlantic.com/national/archive/2013/08/when class-became-more-important-to-a-childs-education-than-race/279064/

Grossman, S. (2013, August 19). For Internet access, rural students have to hit the road. *The Chronicle of Higher Education.*

Kang, C. (2013, March 1). Web access disparity leads to learning gap, study says. *The Washington Post*, p. A9.

Moyers, B. (2013, February 8). Moyers and Company: Who's widening America's digital divide? Retrieved from http://ezproxy.vccs.edu:2048/login?url=http://digital.films.com/PortalPlaylists.aspx?aid=7544&xtid=53088

National Telecommunications and Information Administration, U.S. Department of Commerce: Bureau of the Census. (1995). *Falling through the net: A survey of the "haves and have nots" in rural America.* Washington, DC. Retrieved from https://www.ntia.doc.gov/ntiahome/fallingthru.html

National Telecommunications and Information Administration, U.S. Department of Commerce: Bureau of the Census. (1998). *Falling through the net II: New data on the digital divide.* Washington, DC. Retrieved from https://www.ntia.doc.gov/ntiahome/net2

National Telecommunications and Information Administration, U.S. Department of Commerce: Bureau of the Census.

(2004). *A nation online: Entering the broadband age.* Washington, DC. Retrieved from https://www.ntia.doc.gov/legacy/reports/anol/NationOnlineBroadband04.pdf

Raichert, K. (2013, September 4). "Can gifting computers to students narrow the achievement gap?" *Chicago Policy Review (Online) ProQuest.*

Salpeter, J. (2006). Inside the Divide. *Technology & Learning,* 26(8), 22-28. *ProQuest.* Web. 4 Sep. 2013.

Troianovski, A. (2013, January 29). The web-deprived study and McDonald's. *The Wall Street Journal,* p. A1.

U.S. Department of Education, Institute of Education Sciences: National Center for Education Statistics. (2005). *Internet access in U.S. public schools and classrooms: 1994-2002.* Washington, DC.

U.S. Department of Education, Institute of Education Sciences: National Center for Education Statistics (2003). *Computer and internet use by children and adolescents in 2001.* Washington, DC.

NOTES

Where Will Your Child Be Their Sophomore Year in College?

Home, Sweet Home: Why Didn't You Go to School Close to Home in the First Place?

Written with J. Denise Perrino

College is for everyone, right? Perhaps. A four-year university degree is certainly not the right choice for some students, but there seems to be a lack of connection between action and reality on this issue. Some students go to college at the age of 18 for all the wrong reasons—adult pressure/misplaced ego, peer pressure, "zip code envy," counselor/teacher advice, unrealistic understanding of financial implications—the list goes on.

> The unfortunate truth is that far too many guidance counselors, career placement counselors, parents, peers, and others either explicitly or implicitly pressure students into making the wrong choice for the wrong reasons. The pressure to attend a big name university with tens of thousands of students is enormous.

Sending your child to college at the age of 18 for the wrong reasons can be costly on several fronts. The transition from high school to college can be traumatic. As Brian Harke, associate dean at the University of Southern California, has pointed out, the academic, personal and social implications of attending the wrong college can be serious when the decision is based on "romanticized notions rather than accurate reflections of college life—ideas created by admissions brochures, a campus visit, stereotypes in the media, and stories from family or friends." The prospect of a student then returning home with a deflated self-esteem, who must face peers and explain his failure, is something no parent wants their child to experience. From a parental perspective, spending $20,000 to $50,000 for a year of college expenses, only to discover that your son or daughter passed only a small percentage of their courses, can be a major blow to your financial security as well as a painful family dilemma.

The question students need to ask is: Am I attending college for the right reasons, or am I attending college because of adult or peer pressure or other irrational influences? Harke refers to the nearly 34 percent dropout rate among college freshman as "The Freshman Myth" and contends that many of these students leave during or after their freshman year because they were "overconfident, under-prepared and lacked realistic expectations about college." He further states, "over 70 percent of these students left because they were not prepared for their new social environment" (Harke, 2010).

So why is it that so many students who begin the college experience with high hopes of success return home after just one academic year? The reasons are numerous. Based on a study conducted by Roger I. Yoshino, seven of the 16 most common reasons are:

- Lack of preparation in high school (51%)
- Inadequate finances (39%)
- No clear-cut field of interest (33%)
- Poor study habits (29%)
- Unhappy personal adjustment (16%)
- Lack of academic ability (13%)
- Misconception of what to expect in college (11%).

What is perhaps most interesting is that this study was completed in 1958 (yes, 1958!), illustrating very clearly that things have not changed much in nearly 60 years! Perhaps the time has come to confront this issue head-on.

Adult Pressure and Alternatives Ignored

Too often, there is excessive and unnecessary adult pressure and student ego boosting inherent in the college application process. Parents, students, college counselors and others have told us repeatedly that too many students are expected to attend a four-year college immediately out of high school, even though there are multiple alternative options that can be considered before focusing solely on traditional four-year colleges.

Trade and professional schools and community colleges, for example, may be the best choice for many students, but these options unfortunately continue to carry a stigma as "the places where kids who cannot gain admission to four-year colleges end up." The reality is that trade and professional schools and community college are often an excellent option for many reasons, including financial capacity, family issues, intellectual maturity and academic preparedness.

According to Robert Templin, Jr., president of Northern Virginia Community College (NVCC), "For every job requiring a bachelor's degree or advanced degree, twice as many require more than a high school diploma but less than a four-year degree." (2008)

George Gabriel, vice president of Institutional Research at NVCC, estimates that their students' annual salary upon completion of an associate's degree is between $40,000 and $50,000 per year, and that a large percentage of NVCC graduates pursue careers in science, technology, engineering, nursing, health, information and technology, accounting, and other lucrative fields. In fact, nationwide, community colleges provide 59 percent of the nursing workforce and 80 percent of firefighters, law enforcement officers, and emergency medical technicians (Williams, 2012).

Given these facts, why do parents, teachers, counselors and others press students into four-year college studies when it would be better to consider alternatives, or even a delay, in the application process?

One undeniable reality is ego: If you and/or your spouse graduated from a prestigious university, it may be difficult to accept anything less than that for your child. It may be time to rethink that approach. History is replete with examples of people who attended lesser known colleges and universities and went on to do great things. Does anyone remember that former U.S. President Lyndon Baines Johnson attended Southwest Texas State Teacher's College, or that nationally renowned financial planner Ric Edelman attended Glassboro State Teacher's College (now Rowan University)? Many notable people attended community college, including George Lucas, Hollywood producer; Arthur Goldberg, U.S. Supreme Court justice; Fred Haise, Apollo 13 astronaut; Eileen Collins, NASA Space Shuttle commander; actors Dustin Hoffman, Tom Hanks, Billy Crystal, and Morgan Freeman; public television journalist Jim Lehrer; baseball pitcher Nolan Ryan; businessman H. Ross Perot; and designer Calvin Klein. What did they know that many students and parents do not take into consideration when planning for college?

Peer Pressure

The subject of peer pressure probably needs little explanation, as most parents know how this scenario plays out. Joshua is a junior in high school. He has been taking honors and advanced placement courses since middle school and has been tracked to attend college. Joshua's friends are already talking about the schools to which they plan to apply in the spring. Joshua's list may become excessively long (and expensive due to application fees) so that he will have bragging rights with his friends. When spring arrives, Joshua will apply to his top three schools and a few "safety schools" as back-ups. These safety schools are often excellent schools that get little notice from the Joshuas of the world—they are, in the eyes of the Joshuas—for those who cannot compete at the highest level.

Stopping the glitch.

If the college of first choice does not accept your child, is that such a bad or catastrophic thing?

Joshua waits months to hear from the 10 to 15 schools to which he has applied. Others in Joshua's circle of friends have applied for early decision that, of course, places them in the stratosphere of college acceptance. These students have real bragging rights! They can lean against their lockers and proudly pronounce that they have been accepted by one of "The Ivies." Joshua now feels increasing pressure to not only go to college, but to make a potentially hasty decision and accept the offer of a college that may not fit his interests, lifestyle, personality or, worst of all, his family's financial ability.

Although a bright student, Joshua is a candidate for returning home his sophomore year unfulfilled, deflated and uncertain about his future—part of The Freshman Myth.

Zip Code Envy

When the U.S. Postal Service initiated the zip code system in 1963, it did more than categorize the country by geographic areas. It also stratified the nation on the basis of a somewhat arbitrary number assigned to individual neighborhoods. Those numbers quickly became synonymous with wealth, power and privilege as well as poverty, need and lack of opportunity. Of course, social stratification has always existed in America, but the zip code institutionalized it.

It was not long before parents and students in the wealthier zip codes could boast of primary and secondary schools that were often far superior to many others. The families in these school systems developed an expectation that high percentages of their students must and will go to college. This was fully realized by the middle of the 20th century, when the number of Americans who sought a college degree was one in seven. That number increased to three in eight by the 1970s (Cohen, 1989). The increasing availability of student loans, grants and scholarships propelled this trend during the 1980s and beyond.

Today, it is not uncommon to have a public high school in a wealthy zip code with a nearly 100 percent college attendance rate, for example, McLean or Langley High Schools in Fairfax, Virginia. Ninety percent of all graduating high school seniors in Arlington County, Virginia, go on to attend college (Arlington County, Virginia, Office of Planning and Evaluation, 2009). Conversely, it is common to see a high school in a poor zip code with a college attendance rate of less than 50 percent. Ballou High School in the District of Columbia, for example, sent just 30 percent of its graduates to college in 2010 and

32 percent in 2011 (District of Columbia Public Schools Profile, 2012).

How did this happen, and do wealthy zip code families really need to send nearly 100 percent of their children to college, particularly if the student has not reached the level of intellectual or emotional maturity required for success? If they insist on the importance of a college degree, would it not make sense to consider other options like community college, technical school, or even the armed forces, where higher education is often paid for by the government? If family finances are a major concern, would a state school not be a more realistic alternative, particularly if the student plans to major in a rewarding but low-paying field? A final question to ask before sending a student off to an expensive, private university is: Will these students all become gainfully employed and financially secure when they leave college with tens of thousands of dollars of debt?

Statistically, the likelihood of students graduating in four years is also not high; Stephanie Banchero reports in *The Wall Street Journal* (2012) that "nationwide, 44 percent of high school freshman go on to attend college, and 21 percent earn a bachelor's degree in six years." This begs the question: Why send everyone to college in the first place? Alternatively, the question may be: Were more viable options available at the outset that were ignored by parents and students due to adult pressure, misplaced ego, peer pressure or other irrational factors?

Counselor/Teacher Advice

No doubt, the advice provided by high school guidance counselors, career placement counselors and teachers is well intentioned and honest at its core. However, forces beyond the control of these individuals often lead them to suggest that all students should attend college straight out of high school, regardless of their level of intellectual or emotional maturity.

We spoke with several representatives from AGM-College Advisors located in Arlington, Virginia, and asked if they see clients whose children return home feeling disillusioned or suffering from low self-esteem after their freshman year. In their response, it was clear that planning before even setting foot on campus the first day is key. When the issue of college selection emerges, they engage in what they term realistic counseling, which focuses on intervention early in the process to avoid missteps in the college selection process, effectively eliminating the problem of disillusionment or low self-esteem (Randy McKnight, AGM-College Advisors, 2012). Of course, their clients' investment in good planning minimizes the chances of a student leaving college after the freshman year.

The question arises: Why do high school guidance and career counselors not employ the same strategy? The answer may be that they are simply burdened with too many students. Research indicates that the average high school guidance and career counselor is responsible for 200 or more students. That may be a modest number. Harke has written that in 2008, the California Department of Education reported a counselor-student ratio in excess of 1:900 (2010). That, coupled with the fact that peer and parental pressure are often intense, is a recipe for ineffective decision-making.

When we asked the AGM team what schools can do better to address this issue—that is to say, what they are doing wrong—they responded with several recommendations:

- Look into a variety of options for students and, for parents in the Washington, D.C., metropolitan area, particularly Northern Virginia, avoid the same worn set of default schools (University of Virginia, Virginia Tech, William and Mary, etc.).
- Develop a willingness to learn about the individual student.
- Talk frankly and openly with parents about realistic options.
- Encourage guidance counselors to attend college fairs. This does not occur with the frequency needed to make it an effective tool.
- Openly discuss basic issues such as school size, urban vs. rural setting, and racial/ethnic mix.

These recommendations were made with the full realization that the burden of counseling upwards of 200 to 900 students may preclude some of them. However, in the view of the AGM team, more of an effort can and should be made in this area to minimize freshman dropout and transfer rates. This effort can manifest itself in fairly practical ways by investigating fundamental issues before making a final college selection. The overall cost of the college experience, for example, is not limited solely to tuition, fees, and room and board. Other considerations that should be factored into the equation include distance from home, travel costs, frequency of home visits, transportation while away from home (car, public transit, etc.) and even the cost of storing personal items during summer breaks.

Ensuring Psychological Comfort

Another significant issue to consider is psychological comfort. Parents and students often visit college campuses during the junior year of high school. Both are looking at the overall layout of the campus, living accommodations, the quality and availability of food, access to public transit and other creature comforts. Equally important, though, is how comfortable the student will feel socially. Will he or she fit in? Will he or she feel like the proverbial fish out of water, or will the college experience be socially, culturally and psychologically comfortable? In addition, some fairly simple yet often overlooked issues that may affect whether a student remains in college are geographic location, weather, urban/rural/suburban setting, and school size. These are significant considerations because research has shown that a poor match at the outset often results in freshman dropout or transfer.

Students should do several things prior to arriving on campus to increase their psychological comfort. These may include:

- Using the Internet to investigate student clubs and organizations on campus.
- Taking some time to read about and investigate the faculty. Are they accessible, approachable and helpful?
- Studying the history of the college.
- Using social media to explore the college from a perspective other than its promotional materials.
- Talking to current students. They have the real inside information needed by an aspiring freshman.
- Finding out about local shopping, where to get a haircut or where the movie theatres are located.
- Determining the availability of library resources and locations on campus conducive to study. (Harke, 2010)

Becoming familiar with the cultural, racial, ethnic and gender mix on campus is also important. If a student attended a public school in an urban environment where diversity was the norm, attending a small college in a small town that is racially homogeneous may not be a sound decision.

The Underlying Issues

The Washington, D.C. area is home to a highly educated, highly motivated, affluent population. Nearly 50 percent of adults who reside in the Washington metropolitan area have a bachelor's degree. Arlington County has a completed bachelor degree rate of 69 percent, followed by Loudoun County, 59 percent, and Fairfax County, 58 percent (Fairfax County Economic Development Authority, 2012). These levels of educational attainment are staggering by national standards.

Unemployment in the area has always been histor-ically low, even during the recent severe recession. The value of educational achievement is paramount in this environment. When life's basic needs are satisfied, and discretionary income, time and attention can be directed toward the value of education, the demand and the desire to earn a college degree rises. In addition, the tax effort and tax capacity of local jurisdictions is exceptionally high. It is rare to hear of a school bond rejected by the public. Even in a jurisdiction like Arlington County, where approximately 15 percent of residents have school-age children, school bonds are routinely approved by large majorities.

In this intense, highly driven educational environment, parents, teachers, administrators, counselors and independent providers of peripheral educational resources (tutoring services, testing centers, college counselors, career planning specialists, college finance consultants, etc.) are in constant inertia toward the attainment of college degrees. On the other side of the coin are colleges and universities that are, of course, the beneficiaries of this unbridled push for the four-year bachelor's degree.

There is a college for every student in America, and if your child applies himself to his studies, that college will be a good choice to launch him on to his career. The "first choice" college will seem an irrelevant distant memory in five years.

Nevertheless, according to a 2011 Harvard University study titled "Pathways to Prosperity" (Symonds, et al.), 56 percent of students who begin a bachelor's degree finish within six years. Only 29 percent of those who seek an associate's degree from the more than 1,123 community and technical colleges nationwide complete that degree within three years, and the first-year retention rate for public two-year institutions is about 50 percent (Barefoot). The Harvard study further points out that only 46 percent of American adults who begin a college degree program complete it. This is the worst rate of return of any of the 18 countries tracked by the Harvard study (Weissmann).

Richard Vedder, professor of economics at Ohio University, has argued that the actual value of a college degree may be diminishing and that "if the gains of a college degree fall relative to its costs, people will start seeking substitutes, be it in the form of cheaper degrees or in the form of non-degree credentialing." Vedder further states that colleges seem to be blind to this economic reality and suffer from what he terms "political myopia." In this environment, if the current economic trends continue, Vedder says that an increasing number of Americans "will simply say 'no' to higher education." (2012)

What Does the Research Show?

As discussed earlier, the problem of freshman dropout rates is not a new one. As far back as 1958, researchers lamented this dilemma:

"The problem of dropouts from our schools continues to be a major concern to educators, and it represents a considerable loss of human resources to society. Few questions can be more important to a college than the area of inquiry concerning student separations … The proneness to attend or not to attend college is a product of a complex of social, economic, psychological and educational forces." (Yoshino, 1958)

Betsy O. Barefoot, co-director of the Policy Center on the First Year of College, Brevard College, has stated:

"In the United States, as in many other countries, academic preparation, socioeconomic status, family participation in higher education and being female are good predictors (in aggregate) of whether students will persist in higher education." (2004)

Vincent Tinto, a professor at Syracuse University, has posited that the "commitment" of students to a college or university and to one's personal goals play a key role in the success or failure of a student to complete a college degree." (1993)

J. Richard Hackman and Wendell S. Dysinger, in a study titled "Commitment to College as a Factor in Student Attrition" (1970), also examined the commitment factor in determining whether a student withdraws from college after their freshman year. They categorized students as "persisters, transfers, voluntary withdrawals and academic dismissals." They found that student (and parental) commitment correlated to whether a student "persists beyond his freshman year."

The national first-year student retention rate is not encouraging. Research by Barefoot (2004) indicates "only 47 percent of students entering a baccalaureate institution have graduated from that same institution in five years" and that 29 percent are still enrolled or have graduated from another institution of higher education. The percentages are even higher at the nation's two-year colleges. Overall, the picture is not good. In today's market, students are not known for "product loyalty." In fact, Tinto has pointed out that the reasons students leave an institution after just one year are varied—boredom, lack of academic challenge, poor institutional fit, failure to connect to the campus social systems, financial problems, general dissatisfaction or the desire to transfer elsewhere (1990).

As Barefoot points out, "No American college or university wants to be known for its high rate of dropout" (2004). In fact, *U.S. News & World Report* in its annual college comparisons now includes first-to-second year retention and graduation statistics in its methodology when ranking institutions of higher learning. This is in sharp contrast to the 1950s and 1960s, when student dropout (or "flunk-out") rates were considered a some-what perverse badge of honor.

What Can Be Done to Reverse the Trend?

The dilemma is clear. Students and families are arriving at college and are planning decisions on the basis of some-times irrational, subjective factors. These include peer, adult, and guidance/career counselor pressure, as well as zip code envy, whereby "keeping up with the Joneses" supplants clear thinking. It is then incumbent upon institutions of higher education to take a more active, reasoned approach to attracting students and marketing. Surely this will increase student retention and reduce student dropouts.

What is at stake and what can be done to reduce the freshman dropout rate? First, the very financial solvency of many small, private colleges may be endangered. These institutions often rely on tuition as a major operating source. Public colleges and universities that receive much of their funding from state legislatures are under pressure to increase student retention or face reductions in state aid. These same schools are experiencing dramatic reductions in state funding due to the current recession. Last, as Barefoot has noted, no college wants a reputation today as a place where students are unsatisfied, uncomfortable, disenchanted, bored, unchallenged or left to fend for themselves.

Unlike in the past, when higher education paid little attention to creating psychological comfort for their students, today's colleges are actively engaged in what is now termed "retention management." Some have even created positions with titles like "campus retention director" in an attempt to institutionalize the effort. The University of Miami in Florida offers a degree in "enrollment management"—a growing field in higher education administration (Barefoot, 2004).

As higher education has become more available to students of all socioeconomic levels, races, cultures and life circumstances, the need to recognize the unique needs of these populations has also increased. Many of these students arrive on campus ill-prepared academically, disadvantaged socioeconomically, or simply lacking the study and organization skills and maturity required for a successful college experience. It is not that these students cannot be successful—there just needs to be a more reasoned approach to higher education choices that would increase retention and reduce dropout rates at colleges and universities nationwide.

In his book *Why Don't Students Like School?*, Daniel T. Willingham (2009) identified critical risk factors for minority students, including the lack of cultural capital, family support and academic under-preparation.

Willingham further states that mentors are critical players in the process. His research indicates that in one instance, 23 of 24 at-risk students were able to overcome risk factors with strong mentoring. Even more interesting is that the mentoring does not have to occur in a formalized setting. Professors with a caring attitude, a sense of authenticity and a clear focus on student success are all that is needed. In fact, Willingham's research indicates that many such professors and staff are not even aware that they had served in a mentoring role or that they made a difference in the lives of their students. These unaware mentors can impact a student's life and can dramatically increase student retention. In a speech given at Northern Virginia Community College's fall 2012 Convocation, Willingham stated, "Human connection is enormously important in encouraging student retention and success."

Colleges recognize this, and many have taken measures to address this problem.

Many approaches to increase student retention have been attempted, some with success, some not so successfully. Among these are:

- Working with faculty to help them interact with students on a more personal level to encourage better classroom performance. This is couched in the idea that increased student interaction may result in increased retention because students may feel a closer connection to their classes, professors and, ultimately, the college.

- Creating opportunities for students to develop a sense of commitment to the school through clubs, residential programs, expanded campus orientations, convocations, community service and events that build school spirit (Barefoot, 2004).

- Offering economically disadvantaged students financial, personal and academic assistance through loans or grants, counseling and tutoring/mentoring.

- Offering first-year seminars that bring students together to improve social and academic integration (Tinto, 1993). These courses often focus on study and organization skills, time management, use of the campus library and other resources, and available technology.

• Developing learning communities where cross-curricular courses are taught with students who find intellectual and social unity through small group interaction. This approach not only enhances student learning; it also helps to develop a sense of belonging and, in the end, enhances student retention.

Personal interviews with Carol Muleta, managing partner of Gardener Parenting Consultants, Inc., in Arlington, Virginia, and Drs. Donald and Anne Weinheimer, educational professionals located in Great Falls, Virginia, revealed some interesting ideas (2012). Each of these individuals took a unique approach to the issue of student dropout and retention. When asked the root cause(s) of the problem, their response was to begin the process of instilling the values of responsibility for personal decisions at an early age. Parents should begin speaking with their children about this in elementary school. This will result in a stronger commitment to school, to family life and to work. In the opinion of the education professionals—long before signing up for SAT or ACT classes—students should learn and practice study and organization skills and read a variety of books to set the stage for lifelong learning. These skills are self-evident; however, one aspect of learning is to set goals and to think through actions to obtain these goals. The ability to honor commitments and take responsibility for one's actions is critical. Muleta stated it is not enough to simply say, "I want to go to college and get a good job." Rather, students must consider how going to college fits into a life plan.

The Challenge Facing Colleges

If this problem has persisted since the 1950s, why have the strategies noted above been ineffective? Barefoot has explored this issue in depth and has termed this "a final frontier." In her opinion, rather than focusing on special purpose courses like first-year seminars, colleges should emphasize helping students with core courses like history, composition, calculus and other content areas. More importantly, the format of these courses and the styles of instruction need to be revamped to meet the needs of today's student population.

Evidence is mounting that students today are tiring of pedantic lectures, amphitheater-sized classes and boring PowerPoint presentations. In addition, Barefoot has found that many female and minority students much prefer an educational experience that is "relational, rather than abstract and impersonal" (2004). Given the fact that nearly 60 percent of students enrolled in college nation-wide are female, this is an important consideration.

These factors, coupled with an entire generation of

students who are demanding more tech-savvy approaches to learning, must be addressed if freshman dropouts are to be minimized. It is clear that since the post-WWII era, most, if not all, approaches have been minimally successful.

The challenge facing higher education today is how to increase retention at a time when student choice has exploded, "product loyalty" has been reduced (Barefoot) and the pull of technology permeates all aspects of life. In addition, the issues noted earlier—adult pressure, counselor/teacher advice, the lack of understanding of financial implications, peer pressure, zip code envy—all must be dealt with if student retention is to be improved. Only through creative measures, on both the part of the students and the colleges, can the trend finally be reversed.

Keep several things in mind. First, all of life's decisions do not need to be made by the age of eighteen. Second, failing occasionally is not a bad thing. In fact, if you study some of the most successful individuals in history, failure was the norm for them before they achieved success. I have heard students in my sociology classes at the college state that their parents never let them fail and that they were always cautioned to avoid situations where they may not succeed.

References

Arlington County, VA Office of Planning and Evaluation (2009, August). *Graduation Report: 2005-2009*. Arlington, VA.

Banchero, S. (2012, September 25). SAT scores fall as more students take exam. *The Wall Street Journal.* Retrieved from http://online.wsj.com/article/SB100008723963904441800045 78016624120796346.html?KEYWORDS=sat+exam

Barefoot, B. (2004, February). Higher education's revolving door: Confronting the problem of student dropout in U.S. colleges and universities. *Open learning, 19*(1), 9-18.

Cohen, A. and Brawer, F. (1989). *The American Community College*. San Francisco, CA: Jossey-Bass Publishers, Inc.

District of Columbia Public Schools Profile (2012). Retrieved from http://profiles.dcps.dc.gov/scorecard/Ballou

Fairfax County, VA Economic Development Authority (2012). Retrieved from www.fairfaxcountyeda.org

Hackman, J. and Dysinger, W. (1970). Research notes: Commitment to college as a factor in student attrition, *Sociology of Education, 43*(3), 311-324.

Harke, B. (2010, June 22). High school to college transition, part I. *The Huffington Post*. Retrieved from http://www.huffingtonpost.com/brian-harke/high-school-to-colleg-tr_b_620043.html?view=print

McKnight, R. AGM-College Advisors, Arlington VA (May 2012). Personal Interview.

Muleta, C. Gardener Parenting Consultants, Inc., Arlington, VA (Sept. 2012). Personal Interview.

Symonds, W. C., Schwartz, R., & Ferguson, R. F. (2011). Pathways to prosperity: Meeting the challenge of preparing young Americans for the 21st century. Cambridge, MA: *Pathways to Prosperity Project, Harvard University Graduate School of Education.* Retrieved from http://www.gse.harvard.edu/sites/default/files/documents/Pathways_to_Prosperity_Feb2011-1.pdf

Templin, R. G. (2008, March 23). New reality, new opportunity for higher ed. *The Washington Post*, p. B8.

Tinto, V. (1993). *Leaving college: Rethinking the courses and cures of student attrition (2nd edition).* Chicago, IL: University of Chicago Press.

Vedder, R. (2012, July 11). The college graduate glut: Evidence from labor markets. *The Chronicle of Higher Education.*

Weinheimer, D. & Weinheimer, A. Great Falls, VA (Sept. 2012). Personal Interview.

Weissmann, J. (2012, April). Why do so many Americans drop out of college? *The Atlantic*. Retrieved from http://www.theatlantic.com/business/archive/2012/03/why-do-so-many-Americans-drop-out-of-college/255266/

Williams, S. (2012, September 22). For many students, community colleges offer better deal and faster career track. *Fairfax City Patch*. Retrieved from http://patch.com/virginia/fallschurch/for-many-students-community-colleges-offer-better-deaa0ff85bfaf

Willingham, D. (2009). *Why don't students like school?* San Francisco, CA: Jossey-Bass Publishers, Inc.

Yoshino, R. I. (1958). College dropouts at the end of the freshman year. *Journal of Educational Sociology, 32*(1), 42-48.

NOTES

The Socialization Process
and Its Impact on
Children and Learning

Family, school, peer groups, mass media, public opinion, work, volunteer groups, religion/spirituality, and now social media each play a major role in the socialization and ultimately, the education process. Each of us proceeds through life in a manner we often believe is under our immediate control and influence. It seems logical that the actions we take and the impact of those actions is based upon a series of logical, rational decisions selected and filtered by choice, not chance. Although this seems a reasonable approach to assessing one's lot in life, it is far from realistic, particularly in the area of education. The sociological perspective tells us otherwise.

One of the most dramatic impacts on a child's education is that of the socialization process. The hidden hand of social forces, often beyond our control, guides our lives. The major agents of socialization exert external pressure on each of us. As Charles Horton Cooley (1902) has pointed out, the evolution of "self"—the Looking-Glass Self—emerges from this mix of social forces. George Herbert Mead (1934) furthered this idea by developing the "I"/"Me" dichotomy—the acting or unsocialized self and the socialized self, the self based on standards we learn from interaction with others. This is particularly true during the formative years from kindergarten through high school, but can also take place well into the elderly years. The impact of these forces can vary dramatically from person to person, depending on their life circumstances and social class status. The consequences can be life altering and severe.

The idea that each child enters school with the same opportunities that foster success is not a valid assumption. In theory, most accept this notion. In fact, many external forces have a profound impact on children and teens. Among these are:

- The family from which ascribed status is derived.
- Attendance at a public school or an exclusive, elite private school.
- The composition of peer groups.

- Exposure to mass culture and the media.
- The impact of work and career.
- Involvement in voluntary groups.
- Religious affiliation/spirituality.

Not all children have the same positive family, peer, educational, and other influences. Therefore, the socialization process often results in an environment that is inherently unequal. This inequality has both short-term and long-term implications for the academic success of children. Given an open-class economic system that espouses equality of opportunity, but in practice may foster disparities between social classes, the questions that must be asked are: How does the education system provide the level playing field society desires? What are the roles of school as well as the other agents of socialization in ensuring equal opportunity for all children from the elementary through college years? How can the socialization process help to address the long-standing achievement gap that has confronted public school systems throughout America for decades?

As the primary agent of socialization and the first "educator," the family plays an essential role in the transmission of the fundamental values that encourage and nurture learning in a young child. There is strong indication that children from homes in which both parents have earned college degrees have a significantly higher probability of academic success as well as personal and professional success. The opposite is also true. Children from homes in which parents do not possess a college education will have a more difficult time achieving academic, personal, and professional success. The hand of the socialization process is at work here. The disparity inherent in these environments demonstrates the importance of the family and its role as the primary transmitter of values. The institution of the family in America is the primary purveyor of education as a core value regardless of educational background. For some, it comes by way of birth and privilege. For others, it comes by way of perseverance, hard work, and persistence in the face of adverse economic factors. Regardless, the possibility of academic success is less without the family as a guiding force.

Leaders since the time of Jefferson have known that a strong, educated populace is the foundation of a strong democracy. Absent that, we will inch toward a fragmented society.

Another major agent of socialization is school. It is the primary transmitter of information and knowledge. School systems have assumed other roles and responsibilities that historically had been the domain of the family. Areas such as providing basic needs such as breakfast, lunch and, in some instances, dinner, before- and after-school programs where children spend most of their waking hours in the care of school personnel rather than parents, and teaching morals and values have become a responsibility of school systems. This is a dramatic shift in the respective roles of the family as the primary agent of socialization and schools whose historic role had been to educate. There has been a blur-ring and, in some instances, an abdication of the role of the family in the socialization process.

Few parents would deny the increasing influence of peers in the lives of children and young adults. Although peers can be a positive force manifested in sports, Scouting, faith groups, and other positive influences, they are often a negative influence. The most detrimental manifestations of this are drug and alcohol use, premature teen sexual activity, and other socially proscribed behaviors. In a middle school child's life, peer influences develop in the area of academic achievement. Being ostracized and chastised for "being smart" is a common burden placed on otherwise high-achieving students, particularly minority students. At this point in a student's socialization process teachers, parents, and other adult role models play a vital role.

Mass media has an immense impact on young minds. As with peers, this impact has the potential to be a positive one. Educational television, historical documentaries, sit-coms that portray families in a positive light, and other positive representations of society have the potential to make mass media a positive, productive agent of socialization. However, with the emergence of the Internet and social media, television now has a partner as a visual stimulant of young minds. The culture portrayed by the mass media emphasizes glamour, sexual satisfaction and promiscuity, comedic vulgarity, violence, and immediate gratification of needs. How does a parent cope with the influences of the mass media as an agent of socialization that minimizes the learning process and glorifies the values of instant gratification? Again, the role of adults and the family in a child's life in this environment takes on increased importance.

The role of religion and spirituality in the lives of children and young adults has been minimized by society in recent years. This trend has, along with the previously mentioned influences of peers and the mass media, the potential to send teens astray. The moral compass that religion and spirituality provide cannot be downplayed in today's fast-paced, consumer-driven society. Religion continues to play a role in identity formation. It is a primary transmitter of our core personal and societal values. The founding documents of America contain strong reference to the values of equality, freedom, fairness, and egalitarianism—all fundamental precepts of most religions. Leaders such as Martin Luther King, Abraham Lincoln and others have called upon spiritual values and teachings to awaken the moral sensibilities of the nation throughout our history. Without the socializing influences of religion, the powerful external forces faced by teens—drugs, a sexualized culture, violence, negative peer pressures, and other dysfunctional influences— become more influential. Parents need to be aware of the stabilizing influences of religion in a child's life and realize that religion is not so much a polarizing issue as it is an important element of the socialization process.

As a child matures, work and volunteer groups become important elements of their evolution of "self." Through part-time employment, young adults begin to learn the expectations of other adults outside the context of family and school. The importance of hard work, earning an income, and saving for the future are all values brought to light in a work environment.

Volunteer groups such as Scouting, faith-based groups, sports, and school clubs can also play a role in the socialization process by placing teens in positive peer environments. Mead's "Me" is further developed in these environments.

When this essay was initially written in 2007 as a piece for *Family Magazine*, the Internet was in its adolescent stage and social media was in its infancy. Since that time both have matured to levels unimaginable just ten years ago. The millennial generation, those born from 1982-2004 (Strauss and Howe, 1987), and now the post-September 11 generation have grown up immersed in the Internet and, more recently, social media (Facebook, My Space, Twitter, and a myriad of other social media outlets).

I have seen a complete transformation in the way students at Northern Virginia Community College communicate during my 32 years as a college professor. Arguments can be made for and against social media as an agent of socialization. Those issues are not addressed here. Suffice it to say that interpersonal interaction as we have come to understand it for centuries has been transformed. In fact, the role of peer groups has been altered in a way that now incorporates social media as an integral component of this agent of socialization.

Until recently, social media was not generally accepted as a force in the socialization process. However, the ubiquitous and pervasive presence of social media in society is undeniable. It has transformed the way people communicate and interact. Direct human inter-action has, in many instances, been supplanted by a more impersonal interaction where one may have thou-sands of "friends" via social media. Our very definition of what a "friend" is has been transformed in a world where anonymity and insulting, crude language and, at times, cyber-bullying, has become acceptable. On the other side of the issue is the fact that social media has brought families, friends, and professional colleagues closer than at any time in history. Used in a positive way, social media can be unifying agent of socialization.

The challenges that social media has placed on the

family, the classroom, the public domain (restaurants, automobiles, religious institutions, retail establishments and many other social settings) is palpable. It has brought people together digitally, but separated them emotionally. It has at once brought generations together and it has resulted in what I often term the "New Generation Gap" between the young and the old. It has rekindled old friendships and romantic relationships, while at the same time often resulting in misunderstanding and miscommunication.

It is not an exaggeration to state that the future
stability of our democracy will be threatened
by a widening chasm between rich and poor,
educated and uneducated, employed
and unemployed.

This new form of human communication is still evolving. Its role as an agent of socialization is uncertain, but undeniable. Cooley and Mead would, if alive today, have to re-think their theoretical ideas of "the looking glass self" and the "I/me dichotomy" because social media and the Internet have permanently altered the way we define who we are as individuals.

The socialization process has an enormous impact on children and teens in the context of the learning process. Family, school, peers, mass media, religion/

spirituality, work, volunteer groups, and now social media each play a role in the collective process we term education. Parents must recognize that each of these agents of socialization maximize the role of education in our children's lives. Anything less is an abdication of our responsibility as adult role models for our children and for future generations.

References

Cooley, C. H. (1902). *Human nature and the social order.* New Brunswick, NJ: Transaction Publishers.

Mead, G. H. (1934). *Mind, self, and society from the standpoint of a social behaviorist.* Chicago, IL: University of Chicago Press.

Strauss, W. & Howe, N. (2000). *Millennials rising: the next great generation.* New York, NY: Vintage Books.

NOTES

"Grit": The Missing Ingredient in the Education of America's Youth

What is "grit" and why is it important to the academic success of children and young adults?

Each of us is born with certain factors embedded in our future. Sociologists call this our "ascribed status." These are factors such as the socioeconomic class of our parents, our race or ethnicity, our gender, and other seemingly immutable factors that guide us as we proceed through life.

Thankfully, there is something called "achieved status" that enables us to transcend the seemingly immutable. Some individuals achieve great personal, professional, and financial success in spite of the lot they were handed at birth.

What is it that enables some to overcome obstacles, while others seem held in check throughout their lives because of their ascribed status? If one examines the agents of socialization – family, school, peer groups, mass media/public opinion, religion/spirituality, work, volunteer groups, and now social media – the answer becomes more apparent.

Each of these forces affects the degree to which we do or do not seek to break free of our ascribed status. Some forces exert greater influence than others. Combined, they can either instill what is sometimes called "grit" in an individual, or they can become diluted and ineffective in moving an individual up and out of their ascribed status. Why do some embrace one or more of these influences to become successful while others do not?

"Grit" is the current term often used to describe drive, determination, perseverance, and the ability to overcome social and economic obstacles. It is one of the often intangible characteristics that leaves many adults wondering how a student from an underprivileged background becomes valedictorian of his or her class, or how that same student attains a perfect score on the SAT or ACT examination.

Research is showing that independent variables like socioeconomic status, race, ethnicity, family background, and geography do not necessarily preclude the possibility of academic success. Other factors may play a role in the academic and professional success of an individual.

What Does the Research Show?

Angela L. Duckworth has researched this issue exten-sively. In a paper published in the *Journal of Personality and Social Psychology* titled "Grit: Perseverance and Passion for Long-Term Goals", Duckworth, et al. (2007) hypothesize that in addition to cognitive ability, other attributes may contribute to the academic success of an individual. According to Duckworth and her colleagues, these may include creativity, vigor, emotional intelligence, charisma, self-confidence, emotional stability, physical attractiveness, and other personal qualities. Duckworth theorizes that these attributes may selectively help someone, while others may be important to success regardless of individual circumstances.

She then proposes that the one personality trait essential for a leader in any field is "grit." She defines that term as "working strenuously toward challenges, maintaining effort and interest over years despite failure, adversity, and plateaus in progress." Duckworth further states that the individual with grit approaches life and its challenges as a "marathon." It is the indi-vidual with grit who perseveres and does not give up. It is the person who follows through in spite of obstacles and finishes whatever it is he or she sets as a goal to its frui-tion. Determination, drive, ambition, and perseverance, as hypothesized by Duckworth, et.al. is critical to success.

According to Duckworth, this idea of grit as a determining factor in the success of an individual is not a recent idea. She notes that as far back as 1892, noted social research methodologist Francis Galton studied the career paths of famous people of his time. Galton's research concluded that ability alone was not the sole determinant in measuring success. Rather, Galton stated, "ability, combined with zeal and with capacity for hard labour" was essential to the success of an individual.

A study in the spring, 2007 *Sociological Quarterly* titled "Early Factors Leading to College Graduation for Asians and Non-Asians in the United States" examined the factors associated with academic success among Asian students in America. Among the findings was the fact that the Asian community is not homogeneous. Rather, it is very heterogeneous and it is incorrect to generalize that all Asians excel academically. What the study did find was that well-established Asian groups such as Japanese, Chinese, and Asian Indians surpass other Asian groups like Laotians, Hmong, and Vietnamese. These groups arrived in the United States much later.

Further, the findings of this study conclude that when compared to other disadvantaged minority groups, "they do not suffer the same consequences as other racial/ethnic groups with similar disadvantages." Interestingly, after examining a wide range of variables such as socioeconomic status, two-parent family status, low parental expectations, and low grade point average, the researchers concluded by suggesting further research is needed that goes beyond these variables and that "investigates more deeply the sociological context in which these variables differentially manifest themselves." The strength of the family and the values transmitted from generation to generation—social reproduction—emerges as a significant influence in this environment.

Further study by Terrell L. Strayhorn in the *Journal of African American Studies* titled "What Role Does Grit Play in the Academic Success of Black Male Collegians at Predominantly White Institutions?" (2014) points to "grit" as a determining factor. Strayhorn defines grit as the ability to overcome obstacles and setbacks. Interestingly, his research found that grit is as strong an indicator as one's ACT score in predicting college success.

Thomas R. Hoerr, writing in the September 2013 issue of *Education Leadership*, references Duckworth and a wide range of people from Bill Gates to the Beatles as examples of people who have overwhelming desire, determination, and drive. Hoerr states that Malcolm Gladwell, in his book *The Outliers*, proposes the 10,000-hour rule. That rule, according to Gladwell, is the notion that people like Bill Gates and The Beatles have expended 10,000 hours honing their great success in life. According to Gladwell, those who have followed the 10,000-hour rule go on to achieve great things. He goes on to state that none other than Winston Churchill embraced the notion of grit, although he did not use that term. The quotation, "Success consists of going from failure to failure without loss of enthusiasm" is often attributed to Churchill.

Hoerr proposes that all children need to experience some failure and that the education system must be prepared to provide support to those students in order for them to learn, grow, and prosper from failure. That applies to students who already experience failure and frustration as well as the "high flyers" who seem to excel in all academic areas. Hoerr terms this concept "good failures." Good failure instills the idea that failing is not necessarily a bad thing. It can help an individual succeed later by trying repeatedly to achieve success. Hoerr believes that grit can be taught formally and through modeling by parents, teachers, and others in positions of influence. Again, the primary agents of socialization—family and school—emerge as major forces when teaching resilience and grit. These agents, through the process of social reproduction, teach coping skills and the values associated with not giving up in the face of failure.

An article in the July 6, 2013 *Washington Post* titled "Overcoming Generational Poverty" references a 2013 Cornell University study, "The Role of Planning Skills in the Income-Achievement Gap." This study addresses the issue of a culture of poverty in low-income families and the resulting low expectations and achievement of children raised in these families. Children from low-income families grow up in an environment with high levels of "background noise," an excessive dependency on entertainment as a means to survive, a belief that one's fate has been set and "polarized thinking" that offers no options for academic survival. This is, of course, a recipe for academic failure. The process of social reproduction does not apply in these instances. Children reared in this environment are not shown the coping skills necessary to overcome adversity.

More interestingly, the *Washington Post* article points out that the Cornell study reveals what every elementary school teacher already knows—negative life factors and lack of organization draw a clear line of distinction between students who succeed and those who do not succeed in school. The issue of grit emerges in this environment. The Post states, "It's all about who can persevere through the difficulty of a task instead of giving up. Success hangs on whether a child can, as the (Cornell) study defines it, 'plan in a goal-oriented manner'."

The Cornell study also found that cognitive factors and academic preparedness are not sufficient measures of long-term academic success. The study found that first graders who did not lose their personal belongings, had a sense of the days of the week, and were generally more focused, organized, and aware of their surroundings simply performed better in school. The authors of the study stated, "…We now understand that making sure these young children know their numbers and colors, or learn to read a little better, or spell a little better, isn't enough. Whether they can focus, sit still and plan ahead is a much more fundamental issue."

In a 2014 essay, Temple University Professor Laurence Steinberg stated, "In recent years, experts in early-child development have called for programs designed to strengthen children's 'non-cognitive' skills, pointing to research that demonstrates that later scholastic success hinges not only on conventional academic abilities but on capacities like self-control. Research on the determinants of success in adolescence and beyond has come to a similar conclusion: If we want our teenagers to thrive, we need to help them develop the non-cognitive traits it takes to complete a college degree—traits like determination, self-control, and grit."

Steinberg believes that our high schools are failing to educate and inspire our young adults to compete and succeed. He states that investing in high-quality preschool is important but, in his words, this "is an investment, not an inoculation." The effort we place in helping children during the early years is not transferring to the high school years. In fact, Steinberg states that the various experiments we have tried—charter schools, vouchers, No Child Left Behind Act, Race to the Top Act—have not proven successful. We need more. In Steinberg's view, we need to revamp the educational system to teach non-cognitive skills like "determination, self-control, and grit."

In his book, *How Children Succeed: Grit, Curiosity, and the Hidden Power of Character* (2012), Paul Tough also argues that traditional academic measures of success are insufficient indices of academic success. He argues that what he terms "the cognitive hypothesis" should be replaced with the non-cognitive or "character" hypothesis. Tough states that "success today depends primarily on cognitive skills—the kind of intelligence that gets measured on I.Q. tests." Tough believes that non-cognitive skills are equally important indicators. He labels these indicators "character." These are skills like persistence, self-control, curiosity, conscientiousness, grit, and self-confidence. Himself a dropout, Tough emphasizes the point that studies have repeatedly shown that a strong grade point average is a stronger indicator of college success than is a high SAT or ACT score. This, Tough states, is because a strong grade point average shows time management, organization, and interpersonal skills—all key factors in first-year college success.

Jeff Nelson operates OneGoal, a program in partnership with twenty-three Chicago high schools. The program is geared toward improving student achievement, helping students plan for and apply to college, and pave the way to future success. Nelson describes the qualities and traits OneGoal teaches as "resilience, integrity, resourcefulness, professionalism, and ambition." Nelson has stated, "They are the linchpin of what we do." He refers to this as the development of "leadership skills." This is "grit" in the view of Paul Tough and others.

Interestingly, the idea of grit extends to the worth of the SAT and ACT examinations. An April, 2002 article written by Jay Mathews of the *Washington Post* offers an interesting perspective on the value of standardized examinations. Mathews alleges that while the SAT and ACT examinations are geared to measure first-year college success, they do not measure student intelligence. According to Mathews, a student who scores very high on either examination but who fails in college will shrug it off. The implication is that this student has the luxury of failing and getting a second chance. The student with low scores who fails in college may question whether he is college material. That student may never attempt college again.

Christopher Hooker-Haring, Dean of Admissions at Muhlenberg College, confirms that the SAT and ACT examinations have always been indicators of first-year college success. Hooker-Haring agrees that it does not measure "work ethic, determination, motivation, love of learning, grit, et cetera" (Mathews, 2003).

Concluding Thoughts

Children are influenced by multiple factors as they mature through the learning process. It is difficult to quantify many of these factors. Researchers have given them various monikers. Duckworth calls it "grit." Others call it determination. These factors are instilled in children through one or more of the agents of socialization. The influence of the family, both nuclear and extended, is undeniable. Interestingly, most of the research reviewed for this article failed to point to the family as a source of personal determination, persistence, drive, and "grit." However, the inescapable fact is that children are molded into mature, fully functioning adults through the process of socialization. The family is the primary agent of socialization. As noted previously, the forces of socialization have an enormous impact on the development of one's sense of "self." Absent the influence of the family, the development of an inner drive (grit) is minimized (but not impossible).

The problem facing public and even private schools is simply that teaching self-reliance, determination, and persistence—grit—is not something that can or should be taught solely in the classroom. It is an evolutionary process that begins in the home and is nurtured through the early childhood years by a range of agents of socialization. Schools are only a part of that process. The family plays a crucial role.

Students whose parents both have college degrees and professional careers have an enormous advantage. These students are more likely to have the tools to succeed in elementary, middle, and high school. They are more likely to understand the complexities associated with applying to college, seeking financial aid, attending college, staying in college and, ultimately, graduating from college. These students have parents who have taught them goal-setting, coping skills, and the ability to deal with setbacks. They have been taught "grit."

As adults, we know this to be true. We all want to send our child off to college knowing that he or she is a focused, hard-working, organized, determined individual who will interact effectively with professors, peers, and others on campus. We know these students as self-advocates. Self-advocacy is a critical skill in the academic world. The student without these skills who arrives at college with a very high SAT or ACT score is at a disadvantage, regardless of their test-taking abilities.

There is an abundance of theory and speculation surrounding this topic. At its core, this issue can be summarized in one basic question: Are we instilling "grit" in our children, and if we do, will that improve their chances of academic success?

We look to standardized test scores to decide which students are most likely to succeed academically. We decide who is qualified for scholarships based on measurable indicators of academic success. We send our children off to college often not knowing if they have sufficient focus, drive, determination, perseverance, and maturity to have a successful experience. In other words, we often roll the dice and hope for the best.

The questions that must be asked are straightforward.

Have children been sheltered and not allowed to falter, stumble, and fail? Have we set them up for failure in college? Do we provide children with sufficient coping skills to manage adversity? Have we over-protected them out of love in a world that seems to have become increasingly competitive, impersonal, and "cut-throat?" Have we taught them grit?

These are all legitimate questions that parents should ask themselves, because failure to confront these issues may result in a generation of children unable to lead into the future.

References

Cepeda, E. (2013, July 6). Overcoming generational poverty. *The Washington Post.* Retrieved from ProQuest: http://ezproxy.vccs.edu:2048/login?url=http://search.proquest.com/docview/1398010770?accountid=12902

Duckworth, A., Peterson, C., Matthews, M. & Kelly, D. (2007). Grit: Perseverance and passion for long-term goals. *Journal of Personality and Social Psychology. 92,* 1087-1100.

Galton, F. (1870). *Hereditary genius: An inquiry into its laws and consequences.* New York, NY: D. Appleton & Co.

Hoerr, T. R. (2013, September). Good failures. *Education Leadership, 71*(1), 84-85.

Luscombe, B. (2012, September 10). Failure is not a bad option. *Time.* Retrieved from: http://bit.ly/1jI4MM4

Mathews, J. (2002, April 2). College applicants urged to take cue from SAT scores: Pick school with comparable students or risk falling behind, educators say. *The Washington Post*. Retrieved from: http://search.proquest.com. ezproxy.vccs.edu:2048/cv_790453/docview/409303200/ fulltext/8AD8750FEF7A4F5CPQ/1?accountid=12902

Mathews, J. (2003). *Harvard schmarvard: getting beyond the ivy league to the college that is best for you.* New York, NY: Three Rivers Press.

Nocera, J. (2012, September 8). Reading, math, and grit. *The New York Times*. Retrieved from: http://search.proquest.com. ezproxy.vccs.edu:2048/cv_790453/docview/1038403603/ fulltext/6E4E29E91B6D4EA9PQ/4?accountid=12902

Strayhorn, T. (2014). What Role Does Grit Play in the Academic Success of Black Male Collegians at Predominantly White Institutions? *Journal of African American Studies. 18, 1-10.*

Steinberg, L. (2014, February 13). High Schools Must Demand More of Students. *Valley News.* Retrieved from ProQuest: http://ezproxy.vccs.edu:2048/login?url=http:// search.proquest.com/docview/1497982859?accountid=12902

Tough, P. (2012). *How children succeed: grit, curiosity, and the hidden power of character*. Boston: Houghton Mifflin Harcourt.

Vartanian, T., David, K., Buck, P., & Cadge, W. (2007). Early Factors Leading to College Graduation for Asians and Non-Asians in the United States. *The Sociological Quarterly. 48*, 165-197.

Dr. Ralph G. Perrino

NOTES

The Changing Face of
Higher Education

Headlines during the fall of 2009 in *The Washington Post* proclaimed "A Virtual Revolution is Brewing for College," "Funding Cuts Leave Area Colleges Gasping," and "Rescuing Our Public Universities." Each of these headlines pointed to dramatic changes in the way higher education in America will be delivered in the 21st century. Universities are big business and, as the *Post* stated, "The business model that sustained private U.S. colleges cannot survive" (Teachout, 2009).

That assessment has not changed very much since 2009. In fact, much has happened to increase pressure on traditional modes of higher education delivery in America. The explosion of online universities, Massive Open Online Courses (MOOCs), and distance learning have emerged as trends that will ultimately alter the face of higher education. The January 31, 2013, online *New York Times* ran an op-ed story written by Arthur C. Brooks about online college degrees titled, "My Valuable, Cheap College Degree." These online degrees are called 10K-BA. They are the brainchild of none other than Bill Gates. These degrees offer students a college degree for $10,000 or less.

The Wall Street Journal reported in a story on October 7, 2012, "Texas Pushes $10,000 Degree," that Governor Rick Perry is strongly advocating this approach in an attempt to combat the rising cost of college tuition and student debt. The newspaper also noted that Perry's proposal comes at a time when the cost of an undergraduate education has climbed by 139 percent since 1990, and state governments are spending 12.5 percent less per student in the area of higher education.

The April 30, 2013, *Chronicle of Higher Education* featured a story titled "Major Players in the MOOC Universe," that reported the financial sources keeping MOOCs afloat are not tax dollars, nor are they student tuition payments. Rather, the *Chronicle* story stated that sources as diverse as the Bill and Melinda Gates Foundation, the MacArthur Foundation, Pearson Publishing, Google, Ann and John Doerr, American Council on Education, and numerous higher education institutions themselves—Harvard, MIT, Stanford, University of Pennsylvania, Cal Tech, UT-Austin, UC-Berkeley, and

San Jose State University—are footing the bill for these free online courses. Harvard and MIT are, according to an April 13, 2013, *Boston Globe* article by Marcella Bombardieri, "pouring $30 million into edX, a nonprofit they founded last year to develop interactive classes from those and other premier universities."

These open online courses, coupled with the dramatic increase in online college degrees, has placed enormous pressure on traditional colleges and universities to adapt or face increased competition from non-traditional sources of higher education. Online universities like Capella, Phoenix, and Walden have also contributed to the changing face of higher education.

The Pros and Cons of Digital Education

There are several schools of thought on this trend, whether a 10K-BA or MOOCs. One line of thinking is that these courses offer the poor and marginalized an education, people who would have never received a college degree otherwise. That is a good thing because a potentially uneducated individual now has an opportunity to learn beyond high school, do better in the job market and, ultimately, in life.

The second line of thinking is that this trend will create a two-tiered system of higher education. The poor and the middle class will have access to one level—MOOCs, online universities, and other distance learning options. The upper-middle and upper classes, however, will have the family history, financial capacity, inclination, knowledge, and capability to seek and complete a college degree from a traditional, often expensive and elite private, or even public, college or university. This individual leaves the university with multiple advantages, not the least of which is connections and a recognized school name through which to network and market his/her abilities.

The third line of thought is that a student who attends traditional classes simply has the immersive classroom experience that includes student/professor interaction, student/student interaction, and the development of public speaking, analytical reasoning, critical thinking and problem-solving skills that an online degree in almost any form simply cannot and is not intended to produce.

Last, there is the argument that online learning democratizes the institution of higher education. Community college had a democratizing effect in the late 1940s at the height of the post-World War II GI bill, when millions of men entered college for the first time. Prior to this period, higher education was often the domain of the wealthy in America. It is argued by some that the new era is being similarly transformed by online learning. Now people at the global level have access to the best universities and the brightest minds in America. In her *Boston Globe* article, Bombardieri wrote that students anywhere can now take a course titled "Justice" and a course titled "The Ancient Greek Hero" taught by two legendary Harvard University professors, Michael J. Sandel and Gregory Nagy.

Opposition to Digital Education

In his *New York Times* op-ed story, Brooks reported that Darryl Tippens, the provost of Pepperdine University, stated, "No PowerPoint presentation or elegant online lecture can make up for the surprise, the frisson, the spontaneous give-and-take of a spirited, open-ended dialogue with another person." Brooks asks, "And what happens when you excise those frissons? In the words of the president of one university faculty association, 'You're going to be awarding degrees that are worthless to people.'"

These are certainly somewhat elitist viewpoints from the provost of a very expensive, elite university and the president of a university faculty association. Institutions like Pepperdine have a vested financial interest in maintaining their current status and do not want their student base to dwindle. However, in the context of the national economic climate, where there is a growing gap between social classes and where open social mobility has been reduced, alternatives to a traditional college degree are one possible solution among many.

The Duke University undergraduate faculty recently rejected a plan, hatched by the Duke administration with no faculty consultation, to contract with the online company 2U. 2U's model is small-format online courses delivered in real time. In the words of *The Chronicle of Higher Education* (2013, April 30), "The faculty of Duke University's undergraduate college drew a line in the sand last week on online education: Massive online experiments are fine, but there will be no credit-bearing online courses at Duke in the near future." Those are strong words from a titan in the field of higher education. Duke had followed a series of other colleges and universities who have taken a similar position. On April 16, Amherst College professors voted to reject joining edX, another online provider of massive open online courses.

A May 2, 2013 article in *The Chronicle of Higher Education* titled, "Why Professors at San Jose State Won't Use a Harvard Professor's MOOC," points to a growing suspicion among established faculty about the intent and the long-term impact of MOOCs on college campuses. San Jose State professors have gone on record as simply refusing to use a philosophy course titled "Justice" and taught by Harvard professor Michael Sandel. In an open letter to Dr. Sandel, the San Jose State professors stated: "In spite of our admiration for your ability to lecture in such an engaging way to such a large audience, we believe that having a scholar teach and engage with his or her own students is far superior to having those students watch a video of another scholar engaging his or her students."

The ancients knew something many students
today have forgotten. Reading develops
thought patterns that then lead to writing patterns
that develop uniquely within each individual.

This divide between traditional teaching methods and the new digital movement has also opened another wide chasm between wealthy universities that produce MOOCs in concert with companies like edX, and less well-heeled universities which are required to purchase licensing rights to access the online courses. This fear of a two-tiered system of higher education—one for the wealthy, one for the less well-to-do—has stoked high levels of tension between those who advocate MOOCs and those who are concerned about its impact on the quality of higher education.

The Reality

Joseph E. Aoun, president of Northeastern University, has stated, "We're witnessing the end of higher education as we know it." Aoun's view is supported by many who see the advent of MOOCs as the new frontier that "could transform the lives of people unable to attend top colleges in person, including young people in Third World villages, American working moms, and restless retirees" (Roth, 2013).

People now have access to some of the greatest minds and most intriguing courses in higher education online, and at no cost through companies like edX, Coursera, and Udacity. As noted previously, courses such as "The Ancient Greek Hero" and "Justice" are just a few of the free, non-credit courses available to anyone, anywhere, at any time.

Michael S. Roth, president of Wesleyan University, teaches a course through Coursera titled "The Modern and the Postmodern." Roth describes the course as "an old-fashioned 'great books' course." Wesleyan teamed up last year with Coursera. Roth was a visionary in this area. He realized that Wesleyan needed to be ahead of the curve on the issue of MOOCs. Rather than rejecting them out of stodgy traditionalism, Roth saw it as an opportunity to build on the traditional residential campus experience.

Andrew Valls, associate professor of Political Science at Oregon State University, has questioned the response to MOOCs by faculty members at San Jose State University, saying "Though this is still an experiment, many of the arguments presented by the San Jose State philosophy professors do not ring true in light of my experience… But the whole point of a hybrid, or blended, course is that it combines both face-to-face and online teaching."

Regardless of what people in traditional academia

say or believe, the arrival of 10K-BA degrees, distance learning, MOOCs, and the explosion of the Internet has already altered the traditional concept of going to college. The American rite of passage of leaving home to go off to college upon completion of high school is being challenged by economic, demographic, and sociological factors that did not exist as recently as ten years ago.

The average age of a college freshman has increased significantly. At one time, the norm was to attend college at 18 years of age immediately after high school. That approach has been challenged, and many are waiting to begin their college degree. As is true with many media today, competition from multiple sources of information in the digital age has had a major impact on the way in which education is delivered. Online classes offer convenience, savings, and efficiency that appeals to adult learners, minorities, and new entrants to higher education. Current economic pressures on students and institutions increase this appeal.

Another economic factor affecting higher education is the inability of local and state governments to continue providing funding at previous levels. Schools throughout Virginia and Maryland have had to increase class sizes, reduce access to campus computers, lay off faculty, and take other cost-cutting measures. Overall, state support for higher education has been reduced 10 percent in Maryland and 20 to 30 percent in Virginia. Nationwide, the American Association of State Colleges and Universities reports that 28 states reduced higher education funding during the 2009 fiscal year and that trend does not seem to be reversing.

This has not only affected those states' four-year universities; it has also had a significant impact on community colleges. Northern Virginia Community College, the second largest community college system in the nation with more than 78,000 students on six campuses, has experienced a 10 to 15 percent increase in enrollment and a simultaneous 19 percent reduction in state funding as a direct result of the economic crisis. In this environment, the delivery of higher education to a wider audience gains more traction.

The Future

So where is the future of higher education heading? There was a time not very long ago when distance learning was the new technological innovation. That, too, was looked at askance by many in academia as a cheapening of the higher education system. Distance learning became institutionalized as a mainstream element of higher education. That seems quaint by today's standards where distance learning has morphed into global learning. Those who sneer at MOOCs may well be left in the dust pile of academic history. These changes seem inexorable. All indications point to online universities, two-year community colleges, and other non-traditional avenues such as MOOCs. Increased efficiency, reduced costs, and greater access by more people will become the norm. Students now have access to videotaped lectures, online classes, online syllabi, bulletin boards shared by other students, and free academic materials. Online learning has arrived. It is no longer a joke uttered by academics in traditional four-year universities. In fact, many such schools, some begrudgingly, have seen the future and are moving in this direction. They recognize that it is smart business.

Further, online learning will address several emerging sociological, demographic, and economic trends. Higher education has long been the gateway to success for the upper and middle classes. That gateway has been difficult to access for minorities and those on the lower rungs of the socioeconomic ladder. Online learning has begun to change that dynamic by making higher education available to a wider spectrum of people from all levels of the economy.

The notion that in order to gain a college education, one must travel far from home, live on a campus, and defer income and career for four or more years is an increasingly outdated way of thinking. With the median age of college students increasing annually, and adult students returning to college, the need to create new avenues to college degrees has become more urgent. Online learning options like MOOCS and other digital forms of education remove the issues of affordability and access from the equation. As a peripheral issue, it even mitigates traffic congestion, air pollution, and global climate change by enabling students to gain an education from home.

At the forefront of this trend is America's community college system. According to the American Association of Community Colleges, 46 percent of U.S. undergraduates have enrolled in the nation's 1,123 two-year colleges (2015 AACC Fact Sheet). Since their beginning, community colleges have opened the door to millions who previously had little chance of furthering their education. In addition, they have become a major source of training for many professions, including law enforcement, fire science, health care, automotive technology, and other critical areas of employment. Robert G. Templin, president of Northern Virginia Community College, has stated, "For every job requiring a bachelor's degree or advanced degree, twice as many require more than a high school diploma but less than a four-year degree." Community colleges, long the leader in the area of distance learning, have led the way in digital education for more than a decade.

There is obviously a place for both approaches to higher education—traditional four-year degrees and online degrees and other digital means of service delivery. No one is forecasting the demise of the four-year university degree as we have come to know it. It will continue to play a role in the system of higher education. However, the economic, demographic, and sociological realities of the 21st century all point to a higher education system that will be very different from that which students from previous generations have experienced. This is all good news, for it points to true democratization of education in America.

Some things just never will change. People, including students, need and want human connectedness.

References

American Association of Community Colleges. (2015). *AACC's 2015 fact sheet.* Retrieved from: http://www.aacc. nche.edu/AboutCC/Pages/fastfactsfactsheet.aspx

Birgeneau, R. J. & Yeary, F. D. (2009, September 27). Rescuing our public universities. *The Washington Post*, p. A23.

Bombardieri, M. (2013, April 14). Can you MOOC your way through college in one year? *The Boston Globe*. Retrieved from http://www.bostonglobe.com

Brooks, A. C. (2013, February 1). My valuable, cheap college degree. *The New York Times,* p. A27.

de Vise, D. (2009, September 12). Funding cuts leave area colleges gasping. *The Washington Post,* p. A1.

Head, K. (2013, April 29). Massive open online adventure. *The Chronicle of Higher Education.* Retrieved from http://chronicle.com

Kolowich, S. (2013, April 30). Duke U.'s undergraduate faculty derails plan for online courses for credit. *The Chronicle of Higher Education.* Retrieved from http://chronicle.com

Kolowich, S. (2013, May 2). Why professors at San Jose State won't use a Harvard professor's MOOC. *The Chronicle of Higher Education.* Retrieved from http://chronicle.com

Kolowich, S. (2013, May 16). Yale joins the MOOC club: Coursera looks to translate existing courses. *The Chronicle of Higher Education.* Retrieved from http://chronicle.com

Koppel, N. & Belkin, D. (2012, October 7). Texas pushes $10,000 degree. *The Wall Street Journal.* Retrieved from http://online.wsj.com

Roth, M. S. (2013, April 29). My modern experience teaching a MOOC. *The Chronicle of Higher Education.* Retrieved from http://chronicle.com

Teachout, Z. (2009, September 13). A virtual revolution is brewing for colleges. *The Washington Post,* p. G1.

Templin, R. G. (2008, March 23). New reality, new opportunity for higher ed. *The Washington Post,* p. B8.

The Chronicle of Higher Education. (2013, April 29). Major players in the MOOC universe. *The Chronicle of Higher Education.* Retrieved from http://chronicle.com

Valls, A. (2013, May 6). Who's afraid of the big bad MOOC? *The Chronicle of Higher Education.* Retrieved from http://chronicle.com

NOTES

PART TWO

The Practical Side of Learning and Living

Are Standardized Examinations Serving Us Well?

There has been much discussion and some controversy in recent years about the value of standardized examinations as indicators of college or career success. Questioning whether the SAT or ACT examinations serve the interests of the nation has become more prevalent than in the past. There are a growing number of educators and educational institutions that have begun to challenge the true value of these exams to the student, colleges, and society as a whole.

Further, there is a growing belief that the skills necessary for an individual to compete in an increasingly globalized economy may not be adequately measured through the standardized examination process.

Robert Sternberg (2010) has addressed this issue in his book *College Admissions for the 21st Century*. Sternberg argues that in addition to traditional quantitative measures, an assessment of creativity needs to be part of the evaluation process. Sternberg's thesis is that many students who achieve high scores on standardized exams lack what it takes to be successful during and after college, and that colleges do not always select the best students for their freshman class. Sternberg states, "We should assess and value analytical, creative, and practical skills and wisdom, not just the ability to memorize or do well on tests. And we should admit people on the basis of their potential for leadership and active citizenship—people who will make a positive, meaningful and enduring difference to the world."

Qualitative Indicators of Future Success

There are those who assert that the use of qualitative indicators of future success is fraught with problems. They ask how it is possible to objectively "grade" an essay or some other non-empirical indicator of college success. The answer to that lies in the ability (or inability) of educational bureaucracies to, in the words of David A. Kaplan, "be bolder and unilaterally disarm, at least for a trial period." It also lies in one's definition of "empirical." Of course, the age-old debate among social scientists about whether qualitative research is as valid a scientific tool as quantitative research will always be at the heart of the debate.

Those who argue in favor of the SAT and ACT as objective indicators of college success posit that only an exam that is administered to a large, statistically significant body of students can accurately differentiate between those who are and are not highly qualified. Other subjective criteria like extracurricular activities, they argue, also do not provide sufficient grounds for determining a student's qualifications. They claim that a numerical score is a far more objective criteria and, by definition, a less value-laden way of screening applicants.

Sternberg tells a compelling personal story about how he was branded a loser in elementary school when an IQ test administered during his early years showed low scores. He states further, "As a result of my low scores, my teachers thought I was stupid, and I did too." It was only through the wisdom of his fourth grade teacher that Sternberg was able to begin the process of breaking what he called a self-fulfilling prophecy that haunted him through elementary school. That single teacher set him on a path of success that no standardized test could possibly have predicted.

Sternberg's argument is that human intelligence predicated on skills like vocabulary and memorization is the wrong approach because intelligence is then valued, in the words of David Kaplan, on "analytical abilities at the expense of leadership qualities like creativity and wisdom."

To those who believe it is impossible to quantify abstract creativity, Kaplan and Sternberg respond by offering an interesting proposal. What if students could invent a product, design a costume, or answer a question like, "Was Kermit the Frog right that it's not easy being green?" In their view, it takes creativity to do any of the above. It also takes creativity on the part of the evaluator to see the nuances in an answer to these problems. Kaplan states, "It takes time," something that is not in great supply in today's fast-paced, digital, product-driven society.

...there is a growing belief that the skills necessary for an individual to compete in an increasingly globalized economy may not be adequately measured through the standardized examination process.

Kaplan cautions that Sternberg's approach, while unique, has its problems. "Sternberg's attempt to assess data scientifically is laudable. Still, he wants it both ways: He wants creativity yardsticks to augment tests." Kaplan goes on to offer this possible solution: "So why not be bolder and unilaterally disarm, at least for a trial period?

Let Princeton or Stanford declare that it will no longer accept SAT or ACT scores, instead adding Steinberg's measures. In four years, we can see whether the class of 2015 turns out to be less successful than the class of 2014 or 2016. We won't know if someone doesn't try."

In an increasingly globalized world economy where intercultural, interpersonal, managerial and, in the words of Daniel Pink, "high concept, high touch" problem-solving skills are in high demand, should we not be looking to develop those with creative minds as well as those whose minds are geared toward a more linear form of thinking? We need both, and neither the SAT nor the ACT examinations in their present form address this compelling issue.

References

Kaplan, D. A. (2010, November 1). Death to the SAT! *Fortune*, 32.

Pink, D. G. (2006). *A Whole New Mind: Why Right-Brainers Will Rule the Future.* New York, NY: The Berkley Publishing Group.

Sternberg, R. J. (2010, November 21). College admissions, beyond the no. 2 pencil. *The Washington Post*, p. B3.

NOTES

Bringing Drama
to the Core

A Creative Approach to Teaching Core Subject Areas

Written with J. Denise Perrino

Daniel H. Pink's book, *A Whole New Mind: Why Right Brain Thinkers Will Rule the Future,* posits that the age of left-brain dominance in the workplace and the American economic engine is fading. That is, the "linear, computer-like" emphasis of the Information Age of the 20th century is being displaced by a more right-brain emphasis that will require more "high concept" and "high touch" skills. The age-old dichotomy between left brain and right brain, in Pink's view, will move towards the artistic class—those who can "empathize with others;"

"understand the subtleties of human interaction;" invent and create; and find joy and meaning in the pursuit of life's goals. To some, this may seem like a silly fad. To others, this is a visionary approach that will assure American competitiveness in an increasingly global economy.

Pink thinks the latter will apply. If he is correct, what does this mean for those in education who must prepare students for the world that lies ahead? The impact of such a transformative change will require new emphasis on academic areas that have been, to some degree, sidelined since the days of the Cold War and the space race when public funds were diverted to the pursuit of scientific achievement and military might. Those sidelined academic areas include the performing arts.

Today we find ourselves threatened by an
entirely new set of players on the world stage.
America survived the first alleged threat to our
way of life by embracing cultural pluralism,
entrepreneurship, and innovation.

In 2004, Fairfax County, Virginia, in a unique move, embarked on a new initiative, "Bringing Drama to the Core." The idea emerged from Judy Bowns, Theatre Arts and Dance resource teacher for Fairfax County Public Schools. She challenged Theatre Arts teachers to "employ their natural use of theatre strategies to deliver core curriculum information by writing lesson plans that meet standards in both theatre and the core subject." Bowns also stated, "Using theatre strategies to deliver core curriculum gives the students a new way to learn and 'own' the information that had previously eluded them." This program continues today throughout the Fairfax County public school system. (J. Bowns, personal interview, November 20, 2007).

The mission statement states that the teachers of core subject areas should use creative techniques from the Theatre Arts to provide alternative approaches to SOL instruction while meeting Program of Study objectives. "Bringing Drama to the Core" embraces the idea that the use of kinetic, physical, vocal, and ensemble techniques that teachers use in a Theatre Arts classroom can be employed in the core classroom with effective results. This idea of using "play" to achieve an academic goal outside the realm of the performing arts is a unique cross-curricular approach that has the potential to revolutionize the K-12 public education system in America.

If the world is moving towards a right-brain approach in the workplace, as Pink has stated, then Fairfax County's "Bringing Drama to the Core" initiative is a step in the *right* direction. It may also place Fairfax County at the forefront of this effort on a national scale. The county is currently working the "Bringing Drama to the Core" initiative into the classroom in a number of creative ways. One example is a physics class in which students are asked to illustrate the concepts of nuclear fission and fusion with their bodies. The goal is to employ the use of role-playing to demonstrate technical and scientific principles.

STEM education has once again become the battle cry of those who place an inordinate amount of importance on math and science education in our schools. No doubt, math and science are absolutely critical elements of a balanced education. However, the operative term is "balanced." Balance implies what it says—a correct dose of math, science, humanities, and the arts in public education. Unfortunately, world events and political considerations during times of national stress sometimes overwhelm rational thinking.

Government classes provide another opportunity to employ Theatre Arts techniques in the core curriculum. In the "Mr. or Ms. Foreign Policy" lesson, students are provided with U.S. foreign policy information. They are then asked to create and wear "Foreign Policy Costume[s]" that capture the essence of U.S. foreign policy. A panel of teachers and classmates evaluates each costume on the basis of originality and effectiveness in communicating the concept(s). These two examples demonstrate unique ways in which a student can use the Theatre Arts to achieve a higher level of understanding in core subject areas.

Attendees of the 2007 National Conference on the Creative Economy embraced these creative approaches to public education. Sixty-four percent of conference attendees made two recommendations: "Improve K-12 education" and "[encourage] the free flow of ideas." According to conference participants, this can be achieved by harnessing the creativity of each individual; encouraging risk-taking; promoting tolerance in the workplace and in the community; and encouraging the management and sustenance of an educated workforce.

These recommendations provide the framework for more initiatives like "Bringing Drama to the Core." In a county where 57 percent of its residents work in creative occupations, the development of new approaches to teaching core academic subjects seems more critical than ever.

References

Bowns, J. Personal Interview. (2007, November 20).

National Conference on the Creative Economy. (2007, October 24). Fairfax, VA.

Pink, D. G. (2006). *A Whole New Mind: Why Right-Brainers Will Rule the Future*. New York, NY: The Berkley Publishing Group.

NOTES

Matching College Degrees with the Job Market

Written with Dr. Fred Siegmund

In today's economic environment, students are increasingly focusing on matching the degree they earn with the job market after they graduate. To be competitive in today's job market, students need to graduate with marketable skills. They also must be broadly educated individuals.

Many people still value a liberal arts education because it provides a wide understanding of a range of subject areas and it encourages the acquisition of knowledge rather than information, thereby creating a more well-rounded individual. In the past, employers sought graduates with generalized skills.

In a *New York Times* article titled "Making College Relevant" (2009), Kate Zernike points out that a liberal arts college in Maine is offering free classes or paid student loans for a year to any student who cannot find work in their field within six months of graduation. She also uses other examples such as the University of Louisiana at Lafayette, which is eliminating its philosophy major, and Michigan State University, which is doing away with its American studies and classics offerings. Zernike goes on to state that parents and students are "increasingly focused on what comes after college. What's the return on investment…"

Colleges and universities have always adjusted their course offerings to reflect the needs, desires, and social causes as well as the economic realities of the times. During the 1960s and 1970s, colleges offered courses that addressed environmental, civil rights, women's, and anti-war issues. The subjects may change over time, but the reaction is the same—adapt and modify or face obsolescence.

The key to managing the college experience is to balance economic practicalities with the need to acquire life-long skills. Every year college students choose a major. Selecting a field of study is often based on academic interest and professional practicality. Four years of study in college will go better, and be easier, for those who pick something that stimulates the mind. It is also a good idea to know that some degree programs have an excess of graduates compared to available jobs and job openings. The following will assist in that decision-making process.

Degrees and Growth Rates

More than 1.5 million bachelor degrees were awarded for the year ending June 2007, an increase of nearly 39,000 from the year before. As a comparison, in 1965, 494,000 students graduated with bachelor degrees. Since then bachelor degree graduates show a nearly unbroken increase with each year with few exceptions.

Between 1990 and 2007, 22.5 million people received bachelor of arts (BA) degrees from United States colleges and universities. During the same period the labor force increased by 28.4 million people.

The annual growth rate for people receiving BA degrees during that 17-year period was nearly double the growth rate in the labor force, or 2.21 percent compared to 1.14 percent. The number of people with BA degrees is growing faster than the size of the labor force, guaranteeing that college educated degree holders have a growing share of jobs.

So what does this mean for the student trying to decide on a specific major in college?

BA Degrees in Selected Programs

The increase of new graduates entering the labor force with college degree skills is significant by itself. Consistent and successful work in college correlates with work and performance on the job, assuring that BA degrees in any program improve employment opportunities. Finishing a BA degree has advantages in the job market regardless of the degree program. However, the distribution of degrees by program changes the job market, especially at the entry-level.

For those with specific job preferences and career goals, it is good to know that some degree programs have many graduates, but few new jobs, and vice versa. Given that the National Center for Education Statistics at the Department of Education publishes degree data by program and the Bureau of Labor Statistics at the Department of Labor publishes job data by occupation, it is possible to match degrees with jobs to make informed decisions and avoid surprises.

Matching Jobs and Degrees

A good example is the BA degree in psychology, a major with a degree-job mismatch. There were 90,000 BA degrees in psychology in the year ending June 2007, or nearly six percent of BA degrees for the year. But there were no jobs using or needing psychology skills that did not require a master's or doctoral degree. Therefore, unless a student is willing to complete a graduate degree, there are few job opportunities in the field of psychology.

Computer and information science also has a mismatch, but in the opposite direction. Computer and information sciences and support services had 42,000 BA degrees in 10 programs. Since 2004, jobs needing BA degree skills in computer science are up over 324,000 with expected openings close to 100,000 a year. Computer systems analysts, software engineers, network computer systems administrators, and analysts are in high demand and doing well.

The key to success in life is not to lunge at every get-rich-quick opportunity. The key to success is to methodically plan for the future.

Engineering had 67,092 BA degrees in 34 programs. Engineering jobs continue to grow with almost 149,000 new jobs since 2004 with 48,000 anticipated job openings. Engineering continues to be an employable major.

Communications and journalism programs had 78,420 BA degrees in eight programs. The large number and continued growth of these degrees comes at a time when newspapers and television are cutting back on jobs. Job prospects here are not hopeless because selected media and communications jobs are increasing. There are 40,000 jobs for public relations specialists, editors, and technical writers and there is some growth, but journalism degrees are in surplus.

The teaching profession continues to grow at the elementary, secondary, and post-secondary levels with over a million jobs a year in secondary teaching alone and an estimated 20,000 new jobs a year in recent years. It is a good idea for anyone doing degree programs in social science to consider finishing the requirements for a teaching certificate. Those with BA degrees in mathe-matics (14,954), English, foreign language and literature (75,392), and liberal arts, general studies and humanities, (44,255) may find teaching is a viable and rewarding outlet for employment.

Health professions and related clinical sciences programs produced 101,810 BA degrees in 34 programs. Health care jobs have continued to grow every month right through the 2008 and 2009 recession with regis-tered nurses leading the way and therapy, technologist and technician jobs right behind. There are many more jobs than BA degrees, making health care one of Amer-ica's most employable degrees.

John Bedecarre and Scott Olster state in *CNN Money.com* (2010) that "the number of registered nurses is expected to swell to 3.2 million by 2018, accounting for approximately 581,500 new jobs, according to the Bureau of Labor Statistics." With the aging of the population 65 and older (19 percent in 2030), the need for skilled nursing care and home health care in particular will rise significantly. Bedecarre and Olster also project fields such as network systems and data analysis, software engineering, biomedical engineering, accounting, and auditing will be growth fields of the future.

A Word of Caution

Some in the world of financial planning express the view that the value of a college degree has diminished in recent years. In a *Washington Post* article titled "Is College Overrated?" (2010), Sarah Kaufman raises the question of whether the cost of a college degree is a wise investment. In her article, Kaufman states, "The hefty price of a college degree has some experts worried that its benefits are fading." She goes on to quote Richard Vedder, an economics professor at Ohio University as stating "I think it makes less sense for more families than it did five years ago. It's become more problematic about whether people should be going to college."

Noted financial planner Ric Edelman has observed that in 1970, tuition and fees for full-time undergraduate students averaged $480 at public universities and

$1,980 at private universities. Today, those numbers are $7,020 and $26,273, respectively. Clearly, the investment is significantly more than it was 40 years ago.

In defense of a four-year degree, Kaufman points out that, on average, those who earn a college degree will earn 53 percent more income over the course of their career than those who hold only a high school diploma. The median annual income of young adults with bachelor's degrees is $46,000. For those with high school diplomas, the median income is $30,000. For many with degrees in engineering, computer science, accounting, and the health-care field, this holds true. For others in fields such as psychology, journalism, and the behavioral sciences, this wage gap shrinks. In Kaufman's words, "If you major in accounting or engineering, you're pretty likely to get a return on your investment. If you're majoring in anthropology or social work or education, the rate on return is going to be a good deal lower, on average."

On top of all of this information, the stories of people like Bill Gates, Steve Jobs, Dan Snyder, Michael Dell, and David Geffen—billionaires who never graduated from college—are thrown around daily as examples of how young people can be successful without a college degree. While enticing stories, they are generally as unrealistic as the tales of sports figures with no high school degrees who also become extremely wealthy. Statistically, this will not be the fate of most young people.

A Final Word

News articles like the one noted above question the worth of a college investment. Job and wage data makes it certain college still pays, especially for those attending state supported community and four-year colleges. Matching a program of study to today's job market makes professional and financial sense.

Finding a balance between becoming an educated person and becoming employable in today's consumer-driven economy is no easy task. These goals are not mutually exclusive. Personal, career, and financial rewards are significant and worth considering as one goes through the process of selecting a major in college. The key is to find that delicate balance between practicality and the desire to become a well rounded, educated person.

All parents and students need to keep practicality in mind as they pursue a college degree. In a globalized economy where competition in all fields has become a critical issue, not at least considering the marketability of a degree may be a decision that will have significant consequences in the future.

References

Bedecarre, J. & Olster, S. (2010, September 7). Fastest growing jobs in America. *Fortune on CNN Money.com.* Retrieved from http://www.finance.yahoo.com/career-work/article/110586/fastest-growing-jobs

Bureau of Labor Statistics Occupational Employment Survey. (2007). Washington, DC: U.S Government Printing Office.

Dept. of Education, National Center for Education Statistics. (2007). Washington, DC. U.S. Government Printing Office.

Edelman, R. (2010, October). Are you making this common college planning mistake? *Inside Personal Finance*, 2.

Kaufman, S. (2010, September 10). Is college overrated? *The Washington Post*, p. C1.

Zernike, K. (2009, December 29). Making college relevant. *The New York Times*.

NOTES

The American Community College: A Gateway to Opportunity

As a faculty member at Northern Virginia Community College (NVCC) for more than 32 years, I have seen enormous changes in the way in which higher education is delivered and consumed in America. I have also witnessed tremendous demographic shifts in the composition of the student body at NVCC. This has had a positive impact, and it is the result of three significant developments. The first is change in immigration patterns. The second is increased opportunities for minority and economically disenfranchised students. The third is the rise in the number of female students enrolled in colleges nationwide.

A paper published by the American Association of Community Colleges (AACC) titled "Why Access Matters: The Community College Student Body" (2012) offers some interesting insight into these trends. According to this study, these three developments began as early as the 1970s, when the percentage of women over age 35 enrolled in college grew 67.5% between 1972 and 1976. Nationwide, the number of women in college in 1978 surpassed that of men for the first time. That trend has continued unabated since that time. The AACC study further states that since the passage of the Civil Rights Act of 1964 and the Higher Education Act of 1965, minority student enrollment in college has increased at a significant rate. In 1965, 6% of undergraduate fall enrollment was Non-White. By 2009, that figure had increased to 38%.

Community colleges like NVCC have answered the call to provide an avenue for these new groups to obtain college degrees. It was not always like this, of course. Not very long ago in America only those of wealth and privilege attended college. This evolution has not been easy, but the results after more than 100 years have been truly remarkable.

The Historic Role of the Community College System

Public higher education in America has gone through many periods of transition since its inception. The community college system has played a significant role in that process. It is a uniquely American institution, and it symbolizes the strength of democratic principles upon which the nation was built.

The community college system in America has historically been the gateway to opportunity for millions of Americans. It dates from the early years of the 20th century when the nation was developing the first inklings of a social safety net for all Americans and government was taking the first proactive measures to ensure equal opportunity.

The first community college in America emerged in 1901 in Joliet, Illinois (Stewart, 2009). It was designed to meet the needs of students who desired to remain within the community and still pursue a college education. Joliet and others that followed began to fill the education void that many Americans from lower social classes had historically experienced. Coming out of the Great Depression and World War II, America faced a society that had become stratified based on economic status. Millions of first and second generation immigrants had struggled to assimilate into mainstream society and build the infrastructure that was to become America's urban landscape. They slogged through the economic morass that was the Great Depression, and then went to war against the despotic regimes in Japan, Germany, and Italy. They now demanded a piece of the American dream. Higher education was the ticket to that dream.

Public higher education in America has gone
through many periods of transition since
its inception. The community college
system has played a significant
role in that process.

These economic and personal struggles, coupled
with America's promise as a place "where the streets are
paved with gold," resulted in a realization that the great
democratizing agent – public education – needed to be
extended to a wider segment of the population. Many
Americans find it difficult to believe that well into the
middle of the 20th century, higher education for those at
the lower rungs of the economic ladder was essentially
unattainable. During this time, one in seven Americans
attended college (Cohen, 1989). According to the 2012
AACC report, in the fall semester of 1953, just 15% of
Americans aged 18 to 24 were enrolled in higher education, a figure that increased to 30% in 1969 and 41% in
2009. Until this time, higher education was the domain
of the upper and, at best, middle classes in society.

That trend changed by mid-century when college
enrollment for 25 to 29-year olds and 30- to 34-year-olds
more than doubled from 1967 to 2009. Overall undergraduate fall enrollment in 1967 was 6 million students;

by 2009 it had increased nearly three-fold to 17.6 million (AACC, 2012).

The Gateway of Opportunity

That closed door of opportunity was kicked open after World War II and the G.I. Bill (Cohen, 1989). This legislation made higher education, and its attendant economic benefits, available to millions of individuals. The first true application of the democratic principles upon which the nation had been built changed higher education in America. In fact, by the time enrollment leveled off during the 1970s, three of eight Americans attended college (Cohen, 1989). This was a marked increase and an indication that the community college idea had achieved one of its primary goals—the democratization of the system for higher education.

This transformation had a further spin-off benefit. The ethnic, racial, and gender composition of student bodies across America began to change. No longer the sole domain of the wealthy and privileged classes, colleges began the slow, inexorable process of reflecting a true American demographic landscape. That change coincided with social change in America reflected in the civil rights struggles of the 1960s and beyond. Minority students and women who heretofore had been marginalized began enrolling in community colleges. These students had never seriously considered higher education as an avenue to professional, financial, and personal success. Community colleges changed that dynamic (Cohen, 1989).

Public education has always been looked upon as the place where society would address its social ills and economic needs. We have historically looked to public education to solve racial inequality, unemployment, drug abuse, alcoholism, teenage pregnancy, unequal income levels, and a myriad of other social and economic ills. With the advent of the Jeffersonian concept of a public education system devoid of religious influence, public education in America was off and running. Publicly supported universities created under the Morrill Acts of 1862 and 1890 furthered this idea (Cohen, 1989). By the mid-20th century, the community college system became a further outgrowth of the democratization of education and the use of public education to address the social and economic needs of society.

The Mission of the Modern Community College

Business quickly recognized the value of this. The development of the community college system was also driven by the need for business to have access to a trained workforce (Cohen, 1989). Unlike four-year universities, which have traditionally focused on the liberal arts, community colleges arrived with a very different mission. A burgeoning American economic machine demanded well-trained employees. Community colleges became the vehicle to feed that demand. The quest was not to simply gain knowledge but rather to address the question: How does knowledge produce the greatest benefit to the individual, to society and, ultimately, to business and the national economy?

The mission, therefore, of the community college since its inception has been three-fold. It has served to provide a source of higher education to millions of individuals who previously did not have access to the system due to economic disenfranchisement. As it evolved through the middle of the 20th century, it addressed social and economic issues that the nation faced, and it provided a source of higher education to previously marginalized individuals such as ethnic minorities and women.

Concurrently, the community college system has become a major player in addressing the labor needs of corporate America. Much planning and discussion has taken place since its creation more than 100 years ago regarding its role in society. Those involved pondered whether the then junior and technical college system should offer a 13th and 14th grade to those who simply were not prepared for advanced learning, or whether it should provide a stepping stone to a four-year degree (Cohen, 1989). Business leaders saw value in the first approach. Academics saw value in the latter approach.

Regardless of the original intent, both of these

functions of the community college system have demonstrated that this uniquely American institution will continue to keep the doors of educational and economic equality open to all Americans.

A Final Thought

As the nation emerges from the most intense economic crisis since the 1930s, the role of the community college in America will continue to grow as Americans recognize the economic reality facing them. That reality will include the institution of higher education. For many Americans, the community college option will serve as a cost-effective and practical alternative to expensive universities. The visionaries of 1901 who created the nation's first junior college could scarcely have imagined the ultimate impact of our unique community college system.

By the mid-20th century, the community college system became a further outgrowth of the democratization of education and the use of public education to address the social and economic needs of society.

References

American Association of Community Colleges. (2015). *AACC's 2015 fact sheet.* Retrieved from: http://www.aacc. nche.edu/AboutCC/Pages/fastfactsfactsheet.aspx

Cohen, A. M. & Brawer, F. B. (1989) *The American Community College.* San Francisco: Jossey-Bass Inc., Publishers, Inc.

Gonzalez, J. (2012, February 2). Multiyear study of community college practices asks: what helps students graduate? *The Chronicle of Higher Education,* 1-4.

Mullin, C. M. (2012, February). *Why access matters: The community college student body* (Policy Brief 2012-01PBL). Washington, DC: American Association of Community Colleges.

Stewart, E. S. (2009). A course-based model of transfer effectiveness of community college students transferring to a large, urban university. Unpublished doctoral dissertation, University of South Florida.

NOTES

Community College:
An Option Not to Be Ignored
In College Planning

The following highly successful people have something in common: Hollywood producer George Lucas; U.S. Supreme Court justice Arthur Goldberg; Apollo 13 astronaut Fred Haise; NASA Space Shuttle Commander Eileen Collins; actors Tom Hanks, Dustin Hoffman, Billy Crystal, Morgan Freeman; public television journalist and novelist Jim Lehrer; baseball pitcher Nolan Ryan, businessman H. Ross Perot; and designer Calvin Klein. Each attended community college. What did they know that many students and parents do not take into consideration when planning for college?

The community college of today offers opportunities not available to previous generations. As they opened the doors of opportunity, they also became a less expensive alternative to four-year colleges by providing two- year terminal degrees. Community college curricula also included specialty training or certification in careers that did not require a four-year degree. In addition, they became the stepping-stones to a four-year college or university, where the significance of a deficient high school grade point average or low entrance exam scores was minimized.

Data from the American Association of Community Colleges (AACC) indicates that 46 percent of U.S. undergraduates are enrolled in the nation's 1,123 two-year colleges. These students are seeking degrees and certification in a wide range of fields including law enforcement, culinary arts, health care, technology, business management, and technical trades such as automotive and other service industries. State and local governments are the primary source of funds for two-year colleges. Tuition covers a small portion of the overall cost. The average annual tuition and fees in 2014-2015 at a public community college was $3,347. The average annual tuition and fees during that same time for a four-year, in-state college was $9,139 (2015 AACC Fact Sheet). A student who attends a community college will also be able to save on room and board expenses. The net savings on an annual basis can be substantial.

Financial planners advise that a college degree costing $60,000 or more obtained with full or partial loans is not a very cost-effective planning strategy. This is particularly true in fields such as teaching, social work, health care and other service occupations. Community college can be a very prudent way to avoid financial purgatory when one enters the work force. According to The Institute for College Access and Success, the average level of student debt for all graduating seniors at public and private colleges was $29,400 in 2012. That is an increase from $9,450 in 1993 (2014). That does not include the average credit card debt of $5,000 to $10,000.

Why do so many students who can and should attend community college choose to attend more expensive four-year universities? Much of this has to do with the cachet associated with attendance at a prestigious college or university. Peer pressure and, let's be honest, parental ego also often drive the decision-making process. In a society where financial decisions are often made devoid of rational thinking, emotion frequently supplants sound financial decision-making.

To avoid this dilemma, parents and students should consider several misconceptions and myths associated with attending a community college.

If there truly is a skills gap, then the role of the community college in addressing that gap in an effective manner must be brought to the forefront of the discussion. Recent data from the American Association of Community Colleges indicates that 46 percent of U.S. undergraduates are enrolled in the nation's 1,123 community colleges.

Misconception: Community colleges are the refuge of students who cannot get into four-year colleges.

Reality: Although it is true that students who attend community colleges generally have lower ACT and SAT scores, many students attend community colleges for financial reasons, convenience, family concerns, and job considerations. Many community college students have the ability to attend a four-year college but choose to attend a community college for a myriad of reasons.

Misconception: A university degree is superior to a degree from a community college.

Reality: Community colleges are a major source of training for many professions, including health care, law enforcement, and fire fighting. In fact, recent statistics from AACC indicates that community colleges train 62 percent of health care professionals as well as 80 percent of law enforcement officers and fire fighters. Depending on one's career plans, community colleges can be the best option for many students.

Misconception: There is a direct relationship between the inexpensive cost of community colleges and the quality of education they offer.

Reality: Class size at most community colleges is smaller than at large universities. This results in much more student-faculty interaction. The sole mission of the community college is to teach. The age-old dilemma of "publish or perish" inherent in large universities is non-existent in community colleges. Community colleges offer honors programs for students who want the challenge of increased academic rigor. The cost savings is hardly an indication of inferior education.

Misconception: Students at community colleges are unable to transfer credits upon completion of an associate's degree.

Reality: Recent policy changes at several Virginia state universities virtually guarantee transfer of credits and, in some cases, admission if a student's GPA is at a certain level. In fact, the University of Virginia offers a Bachelors of Individualized Study on the campus of Northern Virginia Community College. This program began in the fall 2008 semester.

Misconception: A bachelor's degree is the only ticket to future employability.

Reality: According to Robert G. Templin, Jr., president of Northern Virginia Community College, "for every job requiring a bachelor's degree or advanced degree, twice as many require more than a high school diploma but less than a four-year degree."

Community colleges have opened the door to millions who previously had little chance of furthering their education. They have also offered a range of professional options at minimal cost. The choice of a community college can be a cost-effective option that enables individuals to obtain two years of a college education while at the same time staying debt-free, leaving assets for potential investment elsewhere. Students and parents should ask themselves whether the cost associated with tuition at an expensive four-year institution is an effective long-term investment strategy. Attending a community college can be a first step toward answering that question.

The community college of today offers opportunities not available to previous generations. As they opened the doors of opportunity, they also became a less expensive alternative to four-year colleges by providing two-year terminal degrees.

References

American Association of Community Colleges. (2015). *AACC's 2015 fact sheet.* Retrieved from: http://www.aacc.nche.edu/AboutCC/Pages/fastfactsfactsheet.aspx

The Institute for College Access and Success (March 2014). *Quick facts about student debt.* Retrieved from: http://ticas.org/sites/default/files/pub_files/Debt_Facts_and_Sources.pdf

Templin, R. G. (2008, March 23). "New reality, new opportunity for higher ed." *The Washington Post,* p. B8.

NOTES

PART THREE

Understanding Financial and Program Options

Understanding the Differences: SAT vs. ACT

In the past, the SAT and ACT examinations differed in several ways. Since its inception in 1926, the SAT tested critical and analytical thinking skills. The ACT, since 1959, was more subject-based and was more closely aligned with high school course content areas. This was often reduced to "aptitude" vs. "achievement." The SAT was designed to evaluate innate ability. This distinction created some controversy, particularly among those who believed that not all teens have matured intellectually to the point where the SAT was a valid measure of ability.

The College Board launched a redesigned SAT examination in early 2016. Much has been said in the media regarding changes to the SAT. Change is nothing new to the SAT. Since the exam first came on the scene, it has been modified more than ten times.

The "New SAT"

Modifications to the SAT will include eliminating esoteric words like "punctilious", "phlegmatic", and "occlusion", and replacing them with words like "empirical" and "synthesis." The idea is to expose students to words they will likely see in college and in the workplace.

The new reading and writing section is more "evidence-based" in its approach. The use of documents like the Declaration of Independence and Martin Luther King's "Letter from a Birmingham Jail" as well as charts, graphs, and passages that mirror what students may see in class, is more aligned with a typical high school curriculum, and is therefore more familiar to students. This furthers the goal of assessing student knowledge of American history, the philosophical underpinnings of the nation, literature and literary nonfiction, the physical sciences, social sciences and other academic areas.

Additional changes to note are that the SAT will:

1. be reduced from a three and one-half hour exam to a three hour exam with fewer questions and more time allotted (70 seconds vs. 49 seconds) per question.

2. be more closely aligned with the ACT exam, which tests mastery of subject material rather than aptitude and critical thinking.

3. include an optional 50-minute writing section. In 2005, a mandatory 800-point writing section was added to the examination, boosting the total score of the exam to 2400. This required writing section added twenty-five minutes to an already lengthy exam. It was almost immediately surrounded by controversy regarding the manner in which it was scored. Many complained that the scoring process was less than empirical and was fraught with inconsistencies. Hence, the writing section is now optional.

4. include Algebra (linear equations and systems); problem solving and data analysis (ratios, percentages, and proportional reasoning); and some advanced math concepts with more complex equations up to the pre-calculus level.

5. no longer penalize students for the wrong answer. In the past, the SAT penalized the test taker for guessing. The ACT has never done that, so this change aligns the SAT with the ACT.

6. include questions that test knowledge of the sciences. This change mirrors the ACT examination which has always contained a required science section.

Frequency, Scoring, and Length of SAT vs. ACT

There is a difference in the number of times the SAT and the ACT are offered and how they are scored. The SAT is offered seven times each year, the ACT six. The SAT is scored based on 800 points per section for a combined 1600 points. The ACT is scored based on 1 to 36 points. The length of the SAT is now three hours with the optional 50-minute essay. The ACT remains 2 hours, 55 minutes with a 40-minute optional essay. Both examinations require proficiency in reading comprehension, math, vocabulary, grammar, and writing.

The SAT and ACT Essays

The essays on both examinations, while optional, require knowledge of grammar, usage, word choice, sentence structure, spelling, and other essential components of writing. Development of a thesis statement with supporting documentation, and a strong conclusion, all critical components of writing, are also required for both the SAT and ACT essay. This is tantamount to the five-paragraph essay most students learned in elementary school. The issues are just more complicated.

Typical writing prompts require that students

reference historical, literary or scientific information. The prompts offered on the SAT and ACT are fundamentally the same. An example of a writing prompt posted on the College Board web site is:

"A sense of happiness and fulfillment, not personal gain, is the best motivation and reward for one's achievements. Expecting a reward of wealth or recognition for achieving a goal can lead to disappointment and frustration. If we want to be happy in what we do in life, we should not seek achievement for the sake of winning wealth and fame. The personal satisfaction of a job well done is its own reward."

This prompt requires the student to write an essay that develops a point of view on this issue. It also requires the student to support his or her position with reasoning and examples taken from reading, studies, experience, or observations.

For those who may have taken a course in research methods, statistics, or any objective science – behavioral or physical – the following prompt may appeal to them:

"Even scientists know that absolute objectivity has yet to be attained. It's the same for absolute truth. But, as many newspaper reporters have observed, the ideas of objectivity as a guiding principle is too valuable to be abandoned. Without it, pursuit of knowledge is hopelessly lost."

This prompt requires some understanding and knowledge of the scientific method and the critical importance of objectivity inherent in the research process. A student could

apply her knowledge of this process to any science that interests her – astronomy, sociology, biology, or psychology.

The first SAT exam in 1926 ushered in an era of
"fill in the circle" education. The most dramatic
example of this trend is the federal No Child Left
Behind program—often referred to by public school
teachers as the No Child Left Untested program.

Another prompt that might appear on either the SAT
or ACT is:

"Martin Luther King observed that the most segre-
gated time in America is 11:00 a.m. on Sunday morning.
Using what you know about the civil rights movement
in America, discuss this observation by Dr. King."

This essay requires a student to develop a thesis statement and provide historical or socio-political insights that
demonstrate an understanding of this period of history.
For a student of history, sociology, or any behavioral
science, this would be an ideal essay to tackle.

The best strategy for any writing prompt is to:

1. read the prompt and do not gloss over
   information contained within it.
2. not oversimplify. Explain your thesis and provide
   literary, historical, or scientific references.

3. freely give your opinion. The use of first person "I" is an acceptable strategy.
4. be sure to use appropriate language, descriptive words, and check spelling, grammar, and punctuation.
5. avoid slang and the use of social media shorthand such as "u" for the word "you" or "btw" for the phrase "by the way."'

The writing section of the SAT, in the words of Wayne J. Camara, Vice President of Research and Development at the College Board, "will be scored using a holistic approach." That is, the writing entry is considered in its totality, and the whole is literally greater than the sum of its parts. The entire impression of the essay gathered by the reader becomes the basis of the final score (Camara, 2003).

Similarities Between the Examinations and a Word of Advice

The SAT and the ACT examinations are one part of the entire college admissions process. Both are examinations that tell you whether or not your child is an effective standardized examination taker. Neither exam will tell you or an admissions officer how intelligent your child is, his or her success in school, or even whether they will have what it takes to graduate from college.

The best advice is for your child to take the test that plays to their strengths. Many colleges will accept the SAT, ACT, or both. Some prefer one over the other, so it is important to check with the colleges before committing to either examination.

When Should Your Child Take the SAT or ACT Examinations?

Northern Virginia Tutoring Service receives hundreds of calls each year from parents who ask *when* their child should take the SAT or the ACT examination. When we receive these calls, we ask a series of questions before making a recommendation. These questions are:

1. Does your child have any weaknesses in the areas of math, reading comprehension, vocabulary, or writing?
2. How has your child performed on standardized examinations since elementary school? Has your child struggled with the examination process in general?
3. Has he/she shown a historical pattern of difficulties in any of the content areas associated with standardized examinations?
4. Has your child exhibited test anxiety in the past when taking examinations?

5. Does your child have any learning disabilities or other educational or emotional challenges that would deter him/her from performing at his/her best on standardized examinations?

6. Have these issues been addressed by his/her guidance counselor to determine whether he/she is eligible for any test accommodations?

7. Is your child currently enrolled in Advanced Placement or International Baccalaureate courses? If so, keep in mind that testing for those examinations occurs in early May. Scheduling the SAT or ACT examinations during the same period may place additional stress on a student.

8. Does your child want to major in a field that requires significant knowledge of science? If the answer to that question is "yes", he/she may want to consider taking the ACT examination because it contains a *required* science section. Although the revised SAT now contains science questions, the SAT does not contain a required science section.

9. Which examination do the schools to which your child is applying require? Some schools require the SAT, some the ACT. To make matters more confusing, some departments within a school may want to see the scores of one or the other. For example, if your child

plans to major in physics, the college may require the SAT, but the physics department may want to see an ACT score with its required science section.

10. Should your child enroll in an SAT or ACT prep course, work with a tutor in a one-on-one capacity, or simply go it alone? Our recommendation is to seek some assistance at some point. Depending on the responses to the questions noted above, most students will benefit from at least some preparatory help. A student with few academic weaknesses and little or no test anxiety can probably get by with several preparatory sessions. A student with multiple academic weaknesses should begin the process of preparing for the SAT or the ACT as far as a year in advance of the examinations.

11. Should your child "go it alone" and prepare for either examination online? That, of course, depends on their level of maturity, determination, focus, and time management skills. If your child has minimal academic weaknesses, has historically been seen by you and teachers as a dependable self-starter, then online test preparation may be sufficient. The College Board has teamed with Khan Academy to offer free online practice questions, free comprehensive test practice, free downloadable

practice tests, and a mobile app that instantly scores paper tests. For a self-starter, this may be all he/she needs to prepare for either exam.

12. If, on the other hand, your child has few or none of the qualities noted above, we recommend face-to-face, in-home tutoring. For students like this, nothing supplants the personalized, tailored approach of a personal tutor. A personal tutor will be able to quickly assess your child's strengths and weaknesses. A personal tutor will also be able to encourage and motivate your child through modeling strong study skills, and he will also help your child with overall time management and organization skills. These are all areas that are difficult to achieve in a classroom setting or online. This all takes place in your home, at your child's school, or at a convenient public location such as a library where your child can ask as many questions as necessary without competing with a classroom full of his or her peers with varying levels of competency.

Why the Change, and What Should You Do?

There has been much speculation about the reasons for the changes in the SAT examination that went into effect in 2016. Some have questioned the advisability of following what amounts to the same approach espoused by the ACT examination since it came on the scene in 1959. Some have called the move by the College Board redundant. Some have speculated that this was a business decision by the College Board, because for the first time in the history of both exams, the ACT recently surpassed the SAT in the number of students taking the examination.

The College Board has taken this one step further. There is also a sociological component to their decision-making process. Standardized examinations have long been accused of socioeconomic and cultural bias in favor of wealthier students. They have also been accused of creating economic inequality and unequal opportunities between social classes in America.

The College Board has openly addressed these issues by doing several things. First, all SAT takers who meet financial guidelines will be eligible to receive four admission-free waivers. Second, as previously noted, the College Board will partner with Khan Academy to provide free online test-prep, thereby reducing the advantage that the wealthy have in the area of private tutoring.

Robert A. Schaeffer, Public Education Director for FairTest, has stated that the marriage of the College Board and Khan Academy will not reduce the market for private tutoring wealthier families can afford. Schaeffer stated: "The partnership with the Khan Academy is unlikely to make a dent in the huge market for high-priced, personalized SAT workshops and tutoring that only well-to-do families can afford" (Education Week, Jan. 2014).

Only time will tell, but it is safe to say that the SAT is seeking larger market share in the highly competitive test-prep industry. Whether making the SAT similar to the ACT makes sense or even offers a clear alternative is something that college admission officers will have to grapple with in the years to come.

Regardless of these changes, your child should begin preparing early to build reading comprehension, writing, vocabulary, math, and test-taking skills. No amount of test prep will overcome a weak foundation. My advice to parents has always been to begin preparation for the SAT or the ACT during the early elementary school years. Preparation for the SAT, ACT, and college begins in the fourth grade! Waiting until March of the junior year to prepare for the SAT or ACT is not an effective, proactive approach.

References

Camara, W. J. (2003). Scoring the essay on the SAT writing section. *The College Board Office of Research and Development Research Summary*. Retrieved from: https://research. collegeboard.org/sites/default/files/publications/2012/7/ researchinreview-2003-10-scoring-sat-essay-writing.pdf

Herold, B. (2014). College Board enlists Khan Academy for SAT prep. *Education Week*. Retrieved from: http://www. edweek.org/ew/articles/2014/03/12/24satside.h33.html

NOTES

Early Decision:
Whose Interests Are
Being Served?

What is Early Decision?

Early admission programs are not all the same. Variations such as early decision and early action confuse students and parents alike. Students seeking early decision generally apply in November and receive an answer within a month. Under this scenario, applicants may submit only a single application to one school. Acceptance by the college is binding. "Binding" typically means applicants promise they will attend the school if their application is accepted. Schools expect admitted students to honor their pledge. Colleges share their early decision lists of admitted students and follow the practice of eliminating them from further consideration. If a student does not honor an early decision, it is unlikely he or she will be accepted by competitive schools. This differs from early action where a student is accepted by mid-December but is not bound to acceptance to the school. Unlike early decision, there is no penalty for not attending the college that has admitted the student. This article focuses mainly on binding early decision programs.

Early Decision: Student Readiness and Family Income as Determinants

Some students and parents think early decision applicants have a better chance of getting into some of the most selective colleges. This notion is controversial. Part of the perception about early decision evolves from the small number of schools that use this mechanism. Approximately 400, or three percent, of colleges offering four-year degrees have early decision programs. These schools are concentrated in the Ivy League and are very selective, expensive private colleges. Since early decision often applies to a group of schools that tend to be ranked among the best schools by *U.S. News & World Report*, the connection between early decision and elite schools may be enough for many people to see it as an advantage.

A November 5, 2011 article in *The Huffington Post* outlines some of the advantages and disadvantages to students of early decision. Among the advantages are: they just want to get the college application process completed so they can enjoy the second semester of their senior year; early decision may afford priority housing preference for incoming freshmen; and early decision demonstrates commitment to a school and may facilitate acceptance of a student who may be a border-line candidate.

Students and parents would do well to remember that early admission implies decision-making for both the student and the institution. Completing the process early is more appropriate for some students than others.

There may be several disadvantages of early deci-sion for a student. Someone may think they know their major, but realize later in the year that their goals have changed. A student may simply change his or her mind about where they would like to attend college. For example, an urban school may have seemed like the right place until a student visits a small, liberal arts college in a rural setting. And the possibility of financial aid may be affected because a college that knows a student is committed to their institution may not give him or her as much money as a school that may be trying to attract the student.

Christopher Avery, et al (2004) has studied and documented the early decision process and has found that colleges that use early decision argue it is not an advantage for admission. However, their research does indicate that applying early admission does, in fact, increase an applicant's chances by as much as a 100-point increase in their combined SAT score. For some students, that doubles or even triples the chance of admission. Even vocal proponents of the fairness of early decision, like Princeton, admit two to three times as many applicants under early as opposed to regular admissions.

Students and parents would do well to remember that early admission implies decision-making for both the student and the institution. Completing the process early is more appropriate for some students than others. Early admission can be revoked if a student's GPA drops precipitously, so an early decision is not a free pass to coast through the balance of the senior year.

One of the arguments against early decision programs has been that they restrict low-income applicants. These applicants often do not apply for early decision because of the need for them to compare financial aid packages from other institutions during the regular admissions cycle. The fact is that early decision programs limit choices for any family in need of financial aid. This inevitably widens the gap between the wealthy and the poor, or at least the privileged and the middle class, and it impacts campus diversity.

In a study titled "Early Admissions at Selective Colleges", Avery and Levin (2009) state that early decision by elite colleges "tends to be captured by students who are well off and well informed" and that "some prominent academic leaders have argued that early admission should be curtailed." Recognizing the inherent inequalities associated with early decision, Yale and Stanford Universities changed from early decision to early action in the 2003-2004 academic year. During the fall of 2006, Harvard University announced plans to end its early decision policy entirely. In 2007-2008, Princeton University followed Harvard's lead.

Harvard's Dean of Admissions and Financial Aid, William R. Fitzsimmons, stated, "We are concerned, however, that even our non-binding program contributes to the pressures and inequities of the college admissions process," Fitzsimmons continued. "Only the more sophisticated students and families look behind the label of 'early admission' and distinguish early action from binding early decision programs. Thus students from less advantaged backgrounds either fail to take advantage of early admission because they are less well-advised overall, or they consciously avoid our program on the mistaken assumption that they will be unable to compare financial aid packages (Harvard Gazette, 2006)." Given the visibility and reputation of Yale, Stanford, Harvard, and Princeton, these developments have encouraged other colleges to re-evaluate their own early decision programs.

The Dilemma College Admissions Officers Face

That was for the years 2003 to 2008. Fast forward to 2009, in the midst of one of the most serious economic downturns in American history. The picture has changed significantly. The October 21, 2011, edition of the online higher education publication *Inside Higher Ed* reports that, "The recession appears to have been very good for the practice of 'early decision' in which applicants must commit to enroll if admitted. Not only are many colleges reporting increased interest from applicants in applying early, but 2009 saw a jump in the proportion of colleges reporting that they were increasing the number of students admitted this (early decision) way." The economic pressure is clearly on colleges to admit a larger percentage of early decision applicants than regular applicants, at the ratio of 70 percent versus 55 percent. *Inside Higher Ed* has also reported, "47 percent of colleges reported an increase in the number of early decision applications they received, about the same proportion as the previous two years." Further, according to *Inside Higher Ed*, 65 percent of colleges that actively apply early decision policies reported that they admitted more students in 2009 than in 2008 through the early decision process.

So although many admissions officers readily agree that early decision favors wealthier students, the economic tug associated with filling classes early in the year is too tempting to resist during economic hard times. Time is money in the opinion of college admissions officers who are increasingly under pressure to eliminate the uncertainty of freshman class size as the academic year approaches. According to *Insider Higher Ed*, "Many admissions officers say they agree with the critics (of early decision), yet can't resist a tactic that allows them to fill a larger share of their classes earlier in the year."

Changes in Early Decision, 2002-2009

Changes in early decision applications								
	2002	2003	2004	2005	2006	2007	2008	2009
Colleges reporting increases	53%	43%	37%	58%	63%	49%	49%	47%
Colleges reporting no change	28%	33%	18%	24%	12%	19%	18%	26%
Colleges reporting decreases	17%	24%	45%	18%	25%	31%	33%	28%
Changes in numbers of students admitted through early decision								
Colleges reporting increases	42%	30%	29%	48%	47%	36%	43%	65%
Colleges reporting no change	41%	44%	22%	31%	16%	32%	26%	30%
Colleges reporting decreases	18%	26%	49%	21%	38%	32%	32%	5%

Source: *Inside Higher Ed*, October 21, 2011

Why Colleges Like Early Decision

Colleges like early decision programs because it is a good way to compete for the most talented students. Early decision eliminates some of the guesswork for college admissions directors. Colleges lose half or more of their admitted students to other schools so early decisions help smooth out the budget process. After all, in the end, operating a college efficiently and effectively is all about business management. In the eyes of many college admissions officers, an early decision student is a low risk investment.

In an interview with writer James Fallows and Bruce Poch, admissions director at Pomona College, Poch reported that early decision for them becomes a measure of commitment. "It's worth something to the institution to enroll kids who view the college as their first choice," he says. "Fewer people are whining about transferring from day one. They turn out to be the campus leaders" (Fallows, 2001).

College admissions officers are less likely to talk about the *U.S. News & World Report* rankings but there is the suggestion that early decision can improve a school's statistics. The *US News* procedures have changed over the years of publishing their national rankings lists of the nation's best colleges. The statistical measures that matter here are a college's *selectivity* and its *yield*.

Selectivity measures how difficult it is to get into a school. A school that accepts one applicant out of four is more selective than one that accepts two out of three. A college's yield is the proportion of students offered admission who actually attend. In practice, yield measures "takeaways;" if one school gets a student that is admitted to several other universities, it scores a takeaway from each of the other schools. The higher the yield and the larger the number of takeaways, the more desirable the school is thought to be. Under this process, early decision provides a way to improve a college's selectivity and yield simultaneously, thereby elevating the school's national ranking. This, in turn, attracts more of those low risk students a college can count on to graduate from their school.

While it is admirable that administrators like Harvard's William Fitzsimmons see the inherent inequality of the early decision process, economic factors often force elite schools to balance principle with practicality.

A Final Thought

Despite Harvard's decision in 2006 to drop their program, and Princeton, Yale, and Stanford's decisions to follow suit, early decision is probably not going to disappear anytime soon, particularly during a period of serious economic decline. Possible reforms would assure more consistent aid packages and limit the number of students accepted. While early admission can help the bottom line of colleges and universities, it holds the inherent risk of creating a two-tiered higher education system that excludes those of lower socioeconomic status. This cannot serve the greater interests of a fair and equitable higher education system predicated on merit, not wealth and privilege.

Selectivity measures how difficult it is to get into a school. A school that accepts one applicant out of four is more selective than one that accepts two out of three. A college's yield is the proportion of students offered admission who actually attend.

References

Avery, C., Fairbanks, A, & Zeckhauser, R. (2004). *The early admissions game: joining the elite.* Cambridge, MA: Harvard University Press.

Avery, C., & Levin, J. (2009). Early admissions at selective colleges (Working Paper 14844). Retrieved from National Bureau of Economic Research website: http://www.nber.org/papers/w14844.pdf

Fallows, J. (2001, September). The early-decision racket. *The Atlantic.* Retrieved from: http://www.theatlantic.com/ magazine/archive/2001/09/the-early-decision-racket/302280/

Fitzsimmons, W. R. (2006, September 12). Harvard to eliminate early admission. *Harvard University Gazette.* Retrieved from: http://news.harvard.edu/gazette/2006/09.14/99-admissions.html

Jaschik, S. (2010, October 21). Early decision bounces back. *Inside Higher Ed.* Retrieved from: https://www.insidehighered.com/news/2010/10/21/admit

Mulvey, Kelsey. (2011, November 4). Early decision: To apply or not apply? *The Huffington Post.* Retrieved from: http://www.huffingtonpost.com/2011/11/04/early-decision-to-apply-o_n_1076093.html

NOTES

Maneuvering Through the Financial Aid Maze

So, you have been wondering about the financial burden of sending your child off to college since that day when he or she entered pre-school. Perhaps you did not think of it that long ago, but now the time has come to face the facts. If you are among the few who actually planned for this event eighteen years ago, consider yourself unique. All too many people simply are not prepared for the financial burdens associated with college. If you are among this group of individuals, now is the time for you to think about financing next year's college expenses.

Several Options to Consider

The first option is available to parents of a new-born—saving through a diversified investment portfolio that allows you to have control over the assets during the duration of time the funds are invested. Working with a financial advisor and avoiding investing on your own will also result in higher yields over a long period of time. In fact, a recent study by Vanguard, manager of $2.5 trillion in mutual funds for investors world-wide, revealed that working with a financial advisor can add up to an increase of 3 percent or more in a portfolio annually. Returns like this over a long period of time can certainly make college planning easier. Keep in mind that, although the stock market has had a difficult time since the 2008 recession, historically the average annual return from the market has been nearly 10 percent since 1926, according to Ibbotson Associates (Edelman, 2016).

A second option is to take out loans, government or private, subsidized or unsubsidized. Although this certainly will place you or your child in debt for years to come, it is one among many options you and your child may want to consider. Again, your child has decades to plan for the repayment of student loans. The key is to attend an affordable school that does not result in excessive levels of loan debt. This may include attendance at a community college where tuition is less than half that of a four year university, and where room and board expenses are not a factor. Modest loan debt commensurate with the earning potential of a degree may be one among many options to consider.

Another option that many parents consider is tapping the equity in their home. Most financial planners will tell you that this is a very bad idea. Taking out a home equity line of credit to fund college expenses certainly keeps your child out of debt, but it also threatens your future retirement not to mention your long-term financial security. Keep in mind that your child has more than forty years to pay off college loans. If you are in your fifties or sixties, your time horizon until retirement is much shorter.

Last, college prepayment plans are an option if you were wise enough to begin the saving process when your child was born. The Virginia 529 Plan is one of those plans. It derives its name from Section 529 of the Internal Revenue Code. Parents can choose between two options—prepaid tuition programs and mandatory expenses and payment programs. Similar to traditional 401k retirement plans, pre-paid college savings plans have tax advantages that parents should examine as they go through the decision-making process. There are also tax penalties if the funds are not used for educational expenses. A factor in favor of these plans is that they do not have income restrictions. In Virginia, for example, parents can contribute up to $350,000 for each child. It is important to note, however, that the program only covers tuition, not room and board. Room and board may amount to more than half of the annual cost of college attendance.

Of course, there is always the option of Federal financial aid. It is also important to note that less than a third of students receive any form of financial aid at all. Maybe more significantly, of those who do qualify for any financial aid, those individuals can expect the aid to cover less than one-third of the overall cost of a college education. So, the best plan is to begin saving for your child's college education when they are born, and continue to do so on a regular, methodical, systematic basis for the next 18 years. However, if you are like many people, this has not been your plan during the past two decades. If you have not saved for college expenses, aid in the form of federal loans or grants is an option worth considering.

If you are among the few who actually planned for this event (college) 15 years ago, consider yourself unique. All too many people simply are not prepared for the financial burdens associated with college.

Federal Aid

Most federal financial aid is need-based aid. To be eligible for need-based aid it is necessary to first file the FAFSA (Free Application for Federal Student Aid) form. Once the form is filed and processed, the Department of Education sends a personalized Student Aid Report, which will include the amount of need-based eligibility for aid. This is simply the amount of money the federal government thinks you can pay out of pocket. Most parents gasp when they see the figure, because the calculation does not take regional cost-of-living into consideration, just raw financial data, nor does it realistically examine the true financial status of many families. To make matters worse, those who save for college may be penalized for saving. Perversely, the system does not encourage parents to save for college. In fact, it may penalize those who do!

Types of Federal Aid

Federal financial aid comes in three types—grants, loans and work study. Most Federal financial aid is administered through participating schools, although some student loans are bank loans. Schools do not have to participate—most do. Students receiving federal aid that has financial advantages like grants or subsidized loans must demonstrate financial need.

Need-Based Aid

Federal need-based aid depends on family income and assets evaluated under the Effective Family Contribution (EFC) formula. The EFC is the expected family contribution to the college Cost of Attendance (COA). The COA is the sum of expenditures compiled from an eligible list of expenditures. Financial need equals COA less EFC. Financial need is the maximum per year of eligibility for need-based aid.

Filing for Effective Family Contribution requires extensive family financial information. There are two forms. The simpler form can be used if income is below $50,000, eliminating the requirement to report assets. Both forms require reporting taxable and nontaxable income net of taxes and a dollar allowance graduated for the number of children in your family and the number attending college. Confusing? There's more… For those with income over $50,000 add 12 percent of net worth to EFC. Families with annual income under $20,000 or anyone in a family receiving federal means tested aid such as food stamps automatically get an EFC of zero.

Grants

Pell Grants make up the heart of federal grants-in-aid, but there are also Federal Supplemental Educational

Opportunity Grants (FSEOG) and two new grant programs only available to Pell Grant recipients: Academic Competitiveness Grants, and National SMART grants. Grants do not have to be paid back so they are always an advantage and a subsidy to students.

Pell Grants go to eligible undergraduate students based on financial need up to a maximum, which was $5,550 for the 2011-2012 academic year. Federal Supplemental Educational Opportunity Grants go to students with the highest financial need up to $4,000.

Academic Competitiveness Grants go to undergraduate students and Pell Grant recipients based on high academic performance. SMART grants up to $4,000 go to Pell Grant recipients for the junior and senior year. Students must be pursuing a degree in physical, life, or computer sciences, engineering, mathematics or a critical foreign language to receive aid in the SMART program.

Federal Work-Study

Federal work-study students work on campus or do community service work while they are in school. No debt results from this aid. Participating colleges administer federal work-study. Compensation is at the current minimum wage and sometimes higher depending on the job. Work-study programs can also instill a sense of self-worth as well as a base of knowledge that will fare well when graduation day arrives. One thing that many college students forget to consider as they approach graduation day is that even the most menial work experience can provide a future reference, basic work experience, and even possible networking opportunities after graduation.

Loans

Some, but not all federal loan programs require financial need. All create legal obligations to repay, which cannot be waived even in a bankruptcy court. Perkins Loans are need-based loans. Perkins Loans go up to a maximum of $5,500 a year with a $20,000 maximum at 5 percent interest for students who maintain at least half-time status. Perkins Loans defer interest and payments until after graduation. Perkins loan payment terms are usually ten years. Students with this loan are also eligible for the Federal Loan Cancellation program if they teach in low income areas or in designated teacher shortage areas such as math, science, and bilingual education.

The Department of Education has two other loan programs, which are called the William D. Ford (Stafford) Direct Loan Program, and the Federal Family Education Loan (FFEL) Program. Ford loans are direct loans because the lender is the U.S. Department of Education whereas FFEL lenders are private banks.

FFEL and Stafford Loans have subsidized and unsubsidized loans. Subsided Loans of up to 25 years have the need-based requirement. Subsidized Stafford loans carry an interest rate of 4.66 percent for 2014-2015. The "subsidy" is due to the fact that the interest rate on the loan is zero for borrowers until six months after leaving school. A subsidy also results if the interest rate is lower than what is available outside the federal loan program (a loan in the market place).

Plus Loans are available to parents of dependent students, but they are not need-based loans. Plus Loans have a limit of Cost of Attendance (COA) minus any other aid. Current interest rates on Plus loans are 7.21 percent for 2014-2015. Interest rates are adjusted each year on the first of July. There is no grace period and payments must begin within 60 days of graduation. Plus Loans as well as Stafford Loans have annual and total loan limits. The limits go up from second, third and fourth year students.

Loans have to be paid back. Calling them financial aid implies they have advantages or favorable terms to students and their parents that are not available else-where. Subsidy comes from a possible lower interest rate and from payment deferrals until after leaving school. Therefore, the financial consequences of loans with different terms can be confusing.

The financial benefit of these loans varies; however, deferring monthly payments until 6 months after grad-uation is worth several thousand dollars of subsidy depending on the interest rate. A student who borrows $4,000 a year in interest deferred federal student loans will have $16,000 of debt six months after graduation. That student's monthly loan payment will be less than the student whose loan payment is due upon graduation.

A Final Thought

The college funding process can seem overwhelming. If you are like many who did not set aside a regular amount for the future through regular investing in a diversified portfolio or a 529 Plan, or if you do not have large amounts of equity in your home; loans, grants and work-study paths may be your best options. The good news is that even in today's economic climate, the options for college funding remain plentiful. Parents just need to know how to work the process. A word of advice is to avoid trying to maneuver through the college financing maze on your own. It is best to seek professional advice from a certified financial planner before proceeding, because a qualified professional will most likely save you time and money in the long run.

Loans have to be paid back. Calling them financial aid implies they have advantages or favorable terms to students and their parents that are not available elsewhere. Subsidy comes from a possible lower interest rate and from payment deferrals until after leaving school.

References

Edelman, R. (2014, October). How much is an advisor worth? *Inside Personal Finance*, 1.

Edelman, R. (2016, March). A resolution worth keeping. *Inside Personal Finance, 22* (3).

StaffordLoan.com. Retrieved from http://www.staffordloan.com

United States Department of Education. Pell Grants Program. Retrieved from http://www2.ed.gov/programs/fpg/index.html

United States Department of Education. Academic Competitiveness Grants Program. Retrieved from http://www2.ed.gov/about/offices/list/ope/ac-smart.html

United States Department of Education, Federal Perkins Loan Program. Retrieved from http://www2.ed.gov/programs/fpl/index.html

United States Department of Education, Federal Family Education Loan Program. Retrieved from http://www2.ed.gov/programs/ffel/index.html

United States Department of Education, Plus Loan Program. Retrieved from https://studentaid.ed.gov/types/loans/plus

Virginia 529 College Savings Plan. Retrieved from http://virginia529.com/index.php?gclid=CKHKmoaOncACFQwV7AodaxQA3g

NOTES

Key Points to Consider
When Hiring a Tutor

"Mom, leave me alone!"

"Sally, you don't seem to get it. You are a junior and this year is critical! What are you going to do next year when your friends are all applying to college?"

"I don't care! Just leave me alone!"

Sound familiar? This all too frequent confrontation can be avoided through some simple proactive steps. Hiring a tutor may be the first step and is tantamount to purchasing life insurance. By hiring a tutor, you transfer the responsibility, burden, and risk to a third party. The truth is that a third party will obtain much more efficient and effective results than most parents can achieve. If you and your spouse work full-time and come home after a long day at the office, doesn't it make more sense to enjoy the time you have with your child rather than engage in the nightly battle of the books?

This article will break down the often-daunting process of hiring a tutor into manageable steps. Many of the considerations a parent must address fall into one of the following categories:

- Do you need to hire a tutor to work with your child?
- What results do you want your child to achieve?
- Does your child need an academic tutor or an academic coach/mentor?
- Where and when do you want tutoring to take place?
- Should your child be tested?
- What are the benefits to the rest of the family?
- What are the qualities of a good tutor?
- Where do you find a tutor?
- What should you expect from a tutoring service?
- What can you expect to pay for quality tutoring?
- Should you take a proactive or reactive approach?
- How can you reduce your anxiety level?

As you work through these steps, it is critical that you set aside the emotional aspects of these issues. This will allow you to use this model to get the objective, unbiased help for your child that will lead to the path to success—and give your life back to you!

Do You Need to Hire a Tutor to Work With Your Child?

The first question that must be addressed is whether a tutor is needed to help your child improve his or her performance in school. As with any decision, careful review of the situation enables you to arrive at a rational decision.

Here are some symptoms to look for:

- The student avoids doing school work at almost any cost.
- Indications of declining grades are apparent.
- The student needs excessive help with homework.
- The student takes excessive time to complete homework.
- You find yourself re-teaching basic skills.
- The student seems frustrated and is inclined to make excuses for inadequate performance in school.

If any or all of these symptoms are apparent, serious consideration should be given to hiring a tutor.

Thomas Jefferson sought the assistance of tutors to educate his daughter, Patsy. He engaged the services of Mrs. Thomas Hopkinson to help raise his young daughter and instructed Mrs. Hopkinson to keep his daughter on a short academic leash.

What Should You Expect a Tutor to Do for Your Child and Your Family?

What Results Do You Want Your Child to Achieve?

When deciding to hire a tutor, parents must first ask one fundamental question: What results do I want my child to achieve? First, lay out specific goals. These goals may include a desired, realistic and attainable grade level, an increase in overall self-confidence, an enhanced level of academic independence and overall self-sufficiency. You may want the tutor to help in one or more of the following areas: a specific subject; special education instruction; general remediation; enrichment to "raise the bar" for a student who may seem satisfied with mediocrity; test prep for the PSAT, SAT, SSAT, or ACT examinations; or to challenge a gifted child. If possible, you should work with your child's school in defining these goals. Take advantage of the knowledge and experience of your child's teachers, guidance counselors, and even the school's principal. Once the exact problem has been identified, working to resolve the problem is much more manageable.

Does Your Child Need an Academic Tutor or an Academic Coach/Mentor?

The first part of defining your child's goals is answering the broader question of whether the student requires an academic tutor or an academic coach/mentor. Academic tutoring should be subject-specific with short-term goals and should be of limited duration. The aim should be to resolve a targeted, specific academic need. This may be a deficiency in some aspect of math that is hindering a student at the higher levels, a weakness in the writing process such as difficulty developing a basic five-paragraph essay, or confusion about conjugating verbs in a foreign language.

Academic coaching, on the other hand, involves modeling and mentoring. Tutoring of this nature will be longer in duration; goals may be less specific and more general. For the student who is struggling with study and organizational skills and who may need to meet with a third party once a week to "touch base" and keep on task, this is often an effective strategy. Draw on the goals you have for your child, and keep this broader goal in mind as you speak to tutors later in the process.

Where and When Do You Want Tutoring to Take Place?

Another consideration is where and when you would like tutoring to take place. You may pay a premium for a tutor to come to your home, or to a public library near your home, but don't forget to factor convenience into the cost. Or, perhaps weekdays are so filled with your job and your child's activities that weekends would be better. Decide when and where you would like tutoring to occur, and then make certain anyone you contact can meet that need. Remember, your time has an opportunity cost associated with it that should not be ignored.

Should Your Child Be Tested?

Among the most mysterious, perplexing, and costly decisions facing parents is the question of testing. The education world has created a subculture that at times seems unintelligible to the average parent. So what is a parent to do?

If a student attends a public school and has been identified by teachers, administrators and support staff as in need of testing services, the answer to this question is generally resolved at little or no cost to the parent. The maze of acronyms that may be assigned to a student is daunting. Public schools are required by law to provide special accommodations outlined in what is termed an "IEP," an individualized education plan.

Such designations can be a valuable asset to parents and students as they maneuver through the maze of elementary, middle and high school class and standardized testing requirements.

Parents whose children attend private school are in a much different position. Most, but not all, private schools do not provide testing services, nor do they address the needs of special education students. In fact, it is commonly understood that any private school can simply turn away a student who may have special needs, something that public schools cannot do. For parents of students who attend private school (or parents of children who attend public school who choose not to use the special education services afforded by the public schools), there are many options in the private sector from which to select an educational diagnostician. These services are often more efficient, sometimes more effective, and almost always more expensive, with costs in the range of several thousand dollars for a full battery of tests.

Regardless of the need for formal, professional testing and evaluation, parents should insist on a minimum of an informal evaluation by a tutor prior to commencing with the tutoring process. This should include a review of any homework assignments, tests, textbooks, and related materials to determine the most effective course of action. The tutor should then establish a plan of action and arrange regular tutoring sessions. The need for formal testing or informal evaluation should be determined through close consultation with teachers, counselors, and other involved professionals.

What Are the Benefits to the Rest of the Family?

Returning to the insurance metaphor, by transferring responsibility for a specific academic area to a third party, hiring a tutor takes the tension out of the relationship a parent may have with their child. Goals you set for a tutor should have far-reaching implications for the entire family, not just your child. Bringing peace back to the family by ending the battle of the books is a worthwhile reason to hire a qualified tutor.

How Do You Find and Choose a Tutor?

What Are the Qualities of a Good Tutor?

Now that you know what you would like your child to learn from a tutor, it is time to find a good tutor. To begin the process, you need to know what to look for. First and foremost, a tutor should enjoy the company of children and young adults. They should also have a little "kid" left in them. Any service that does not clearly exhibit enthusiasm for children and their academic success should be avoided. The tutor should:

- Come to all sessions regularly and on time.
- Be organized (why would a disorganized

student get organized if his/her tutor does not demonstrate this trait?).
- Set clear goals and expectations.
- Work at a level that is comfortable for the student.
- Not do the work for the student.
- Teach independent learning skills.

Of course, any tutor who works with a student should be technically qualified to perform the task at hand. This should entail a minimum of a bachelor's degree. Should you hire a tutor who does not possess state teaching certification or an education background? The answer to that question lies in the nature of the problem. If a child is in the elementary or middle school years, it is best to hire a teaching professional who has knowledge of and experience with those age groups. That rule generally does not have to apply when the issue is high school and college level math, science, languages, and research/writing. Eliminating non-teachers in these areas removes a large, highly qualified segment of the population from your pool of options.

Where Do You Find a Tutor?
Exploring the range of options available to you is a critical factor. Options available to parents include large commercial franchises, private independent tutoring services, after-school programs, college tutoring centers,

on-line tutoring, SAT prep centers, no-cost tutoring at schools that qualify under federal "No Child Left Behind" guidelines, and independent tutors.

Each of these options varies in:

- **Reliability.** A company is likely to be more reliable than a college student looking to make extra money
- **Personalization.** Smaller companies and individual tutors may be more likely to cater to your child's specific needs, rather than a program they developed
- **Accessibility.** Working with a company gives you additional accountability and support staff to talk to if you ever have a problem.

In arriving at a decision, consider more than just the cost of tutoring (see "What Can I Expect to Pay?" for more information). Quality, convenience, dependability and flexibility are all factors you should include. Although tutoring can be expensive, the opportunity costs of a wrong decision based purely on an hourly rate can be disastrous. Parents need to balance cost and cost-effectiveness; both play a crucial role in this decision.

What Should You Expect From a Tutoring Service?

Any tutoring service that is being seriously considered should provide prompt, reliable, efficient and effective service. It should also be responsive, accountable, and committed to the education process. It should provide qualified, compassionate, caring, and knowledgeable tutors who are motivators as well as educators. Tutors should suggest specific strategies to resolve a problem and offer guidance through the process of identifying a solution. Any tutoring service that is in serious consideration should demonstrate honesty and a sense of professional ethics and should freely offer to provide references.

What Can You Expect to Pay for Quality Tutoring?

Last, of course, are the logistics of tutoring and costs and contractual obligations associated with the process. Considerations such as how far one is willing to travel to a tutoring service and whether a service is willing to come to your home are quality of life factors that should not be discounted. In today's hectic world in which both parents often work, the convenience of a tutor coming to the home is something that should be factored in. The cost for this convenience may well be worth it in the long term.

Costs for tutoring vary significantly, depending on the model chosen. Options include teachers and individuals who may be tutoring independently. Depending on age and experience, you might pay anywhere from $15 per hour for a high school kid who knows a little more than your child to $60 per hour for someone with a master's degree who is providing her own materials. Other possibilities are large national chains, which might be more expensive and less flexible, yet offer reliability, accessibility, and consistency. With a small independent tutoring service you can expect to pay between $70 to $95 per hour, reflecting a pre-screened, high-quality tutor, as well as overhead office and advertising costs. High school or college tutoring centers might even be free, but be sure to look at the background and level of commitment of the tutors. Costs will vary by subject, with math and science tutors commanding the higher hourly rates.

Each of these models has positive and negative aspects. Among these are the contractual obligations of the arrangement. Many firms require a long-term contract commitment. Others offer more open-ended contracts, which assume that when the client, in consultation with the tutor, teachers, and the tutoring service, determines that tutoring is no longer needed, that the contractual obligation should cease. The choice should be driven by the specific needs of the student and the family, not by the bottom line of the tutoring service.

A checklist of questions you should ask a tutor/ tutoring service may include:

- How do you select your tutors? What kind of expertise and experience do tutors have in their subject area?

- What happens if I want to change tutors?
- Where does tutoring take place?
- What is the cost of tutoring? Are there any administrative fees?
- Does the contract obligate me to a long-term commitment?
- Can you provide references?

The Why and How of Being Proactive

Should You Take a Proactive or Reactive Approach?
To maximize the benefit of tutoring and academic coaching, don't wait for bad grades and reports from teachers. Keep an eye out for the following signs that may be more subtle indicators of an impending problem: frustration with school, work consistently avoided, work not turned in, and unwillingness to wake up in the morning. Most importantly, be alert to signs of exhaustion and depression. These often manifest themselves in subtle ways in teens. A keen parental eye should spot this early.

You can also take proactive steps in your everyday behavior at home by modeling the importance of learning. Make learning a priority and part of the family culture. Teach by modeling and do not accept below par, self-defeatist attitudes. Remember, kids often mimic what they see at home. The family, as the first socializing agent, is the first line of defense against an increasingly intrusive popular culture. Parents who are tuned into their children's academic, emotional, and social needs and who are proactive in addressing those needs generally will have far happier, more successful children.

> Among the most mysterious, perplexing, and costly decisions facing parents is the question of testing. The education world has created a subculture that at times seems unintelligible to the average parent. So what is a parent to do?

It's not ideal, but sometimes grades fall suddenly and we, as parents, are caught off guard. Don't panic! Follow the suggestions outlined in this article, but be realistic. Tutoring is not the same thing as a miracle. But it is a key component to turning academic performance around and improving your child's general attitude toward school. That, of course, is the first step toward resolution of the problem.

These key points to consider when hiring a tutor are important to thoroughly review before signing on the dotted line with any firm. A methodical, rational approach devoid of emotion will result in a cost-effective decision that addresses the core problem. Only then can a student begin to enjoy the academic success he or she deserves. Parents then can remove themselves from the academically volatile situation with their children and enjoy family time once again!

You can also take proactive steps in your everyday behavior at home by modeling the importance of learning. Make learning a priority and part of the family culture. Teach by modeling and do not accept below par, self-defeatist attitudes. Remember, kids often mimic what they see at home. The family, as the first socializing agent, is the first line of defense against an increasingly intrusive popular culture.

How Can You Reduce Your Anxiety Level?

This may be the ultimate question. Parents wrestle with it constantly and kids pick up on parental vibes, which only exacerbates the problem. The most important thing to remember is that your child will be successful in spite of himself! Most of the short-term, seemingly insurmountable obstacles your child faces as he or she progresses through elementary, middle, and high school will, in most instances, fall by the wayside as they grow to adulthood. After all, your child has caring, educated parents who will do whatever it takes to help them succeed, right? The likelihood of failure is slim, particularly in families where both parents are college educated. Research supports this assertion.

In addition, keep several things in mind. First, all of life's decisions do not need to be made by the age of eighteen. Second, failing occasionally is not a bad thing. In fact, if you study some of the most successful individuals in history, failure was the norm for them before they achieved success. Third, if your child does not get accepted by the college of first choice, is that such a bad or catastrophic thing? You know that next year they will be studying in some college somewhere. There is a college for every student somewhere in America, and if your child applies himself to his studies, that college will be a good choice to launch him on to his career. The first choice college will seem an irrelevant and distant memory in five years. And, let's face it, when your daughter calls home a month after arriving on campus and tells you she loves college, finds her classes motivating and inspiring, and enjoys living with her roommate and, oh, by the way, has to run because she is supposed to meet a study group in ten minutes, isn't that exactly what you wanted to hear?

So, relax, be the best, most supportive parent you can be, but do it in a non-intrusive manner that is acceptable to your teenager. In most instances, any advice you offer will be rejected outright, even if you do have a doctorate in counseling psychology—because you are their parent! At some point in their adult life, they will realize you actually do have a brain and they will then ask for your advice. Until then, advise discreetly from the sidelines. That is the first step toward reducing your anxiety level—and theirs.

NOTES

PART FOUR

Entrepreneurship

The Importance of Intercultural Communication In the World of Business

In William Lederer and Eugene Burdick's landmark 1958 Novel, *The Ugly American*, a fictional journalist from Burma writes:

> For some reason…the Americans I meet
> in my country are not the same as the ones
> I knew in the United States. A mysterious
> change seems to come over Americans
> when they go to a foreign land. They isolate
> themselves socially. They live pretentiously.
> They're loud and ostentatious.

This prescient novel portrays Americans as arrogant and ethnocentric when living in cultures that embrace entirely different sets of cultural values. The novel had a major impact on Americans' perceptions of themselves and prompted then President Dwight D. Eisenhower to modify his foreign aid programs in Asia.

We find ourselves in the same predicament 50 years later in the Middle East. How did Americans get into this pattern of offensive behavior, and what should we do to resolve the problem? This question is particularly critical in the world of business where cultural slights and blatant insults can result in corporate losses.

Respecting others' values in all cultural settings is critical, but it is particularly important in the business world. This respect can manifest itself in everyday things such as dress, mannerisms, gestures, eye contact and hand shaking. It is also apparent in more critical areas such as sales, monetary transactions, religious sensitivities, governmental and political processes, among others.

That begs the question: How does someone from any culture, not just American, confront intercultural communication in the business world?

Small Group Dynamics and Culture

Given the fact that a sizable number of daily, routine business transactions occur between two or three people, an awareness of cultural, religious and social customs, norms, folkways, belief systems and, in some cases, mores are at play. Failure to stay abreast of cultural systems that are steeped in generations of a given culture may hinder present and future business transactions.

Ethnocentrism and Business

People are often constrained by "perceptual blinders" that develop over time. These social constructs hinder creativity and open thinking. In the world of business, this often-damaging tendency can negatively affect cross-cultural communications to the point where business transactions may be hindered or even lost. Keeping an open mind about and respecting other cultures is critical.

Respect for Cultural Values = Profitability

Of course, most would agree that not respecting the values and culture of others in today's global economy would be imprudent at best. Those who see the importance of this will prosper. Those who do not or will not will be swallowed in a sea of competition. In his recent book, *A Whole New Mind: Why Right Brain Thinkers Will Rule the Future,* Daniel Pink posits that those with "high concept," "high touch" aptitudes who see the importance of empathy as an element of leadership will thrive in what he terms the Conceptual Age. If those in positions of intercultural communications use such skills to work within the parameters of their business partners' culture, they will enhance the net financial impact of a business's bottom line.

Lederer and Burdick's novel, written in the 1950s, does not have to be the path to the future for American international business interests. A relatively simple awareness of others' cultures will help to prevent misunderstandings and increase business profitability.

Respecting others' values in all cultural settings is critical, but it is particularly important in the business world. This respect can manifest itself in everyday things such as dress, mannerisms, gestures, eye contact and hand shaking.

References

Lederer, W. J. & Burdick, E. (1958). *The Ugly American.* New York, NY: Random House Publishing Group.

Pink, D. (2006). *A Whole New Mind: Why Right Brain Thinkers Will Rule the Future.* New York, NY: Riverhead Trade.

NOTES

Starting Your Own Business

"Being an entrepreneur is not for the faint of heart!" This is a refrain often stated when challenges arise while conducting business at Northern Virginia Tutoring Service. The challenges associated with operating one's own business are at once exhilarating and daunting. In order to manage the daily affairs of a small business, several important legal and administrative issues and processes must be addressed. In addition, there are many skills, as well as personal characteristics and values that must be in place.

Legal, Administrative and Financial Issues

Starting your own business is not nearly as glamorous as the ads on television or in magazines make it seem. There are a multitude of legal, administrative, and financial issues that must be faced at the outset.

The first step is to make a determination regarding the *proper legal status* of your business. Should the business be a sole proprietorship, an S-Corp., a limited liability company? Each of these legal models offers advantages and disadvantages too numerous to detail here. Seeking legal advice from a qualified attorney whose sole interest is business law is critical. This decision has significant tax implications as well as corporate liability implications.

The issue of *effective administration* becomes critical at this juncture. Decisions such as the need for office space, supplies, equipment, furnishings, and technology must be made. Such decisions are often made in a vacuum by well-intentioned people who regret their mistakes at a later date. It is often worth seeking the services of a management consultant to assist in these decisions.

Financial issues are one of the most intimidating things facing any small business owner. The small business owner must address and answer questions such as: Do I have sufficient capital on hand to start the process? If not, where should I seek start-up capital? Does my enterprise require that I find commercial office / retail space immediately? Can I begin operations from home? How do I market my product or service? What are my capital equipment needs? Where and how do I advertise? These and other financial issues and decisions are important because failure to address these issues or making the wrong decision may result in early business failure.

Skills

The skills necessary to operate a business efficiently and effectively are numerous, some tangible, some intangible. Some skills will never be learned in a classroom, but come from life experience as well as trial and error.

Interpersonal and public speaking skills are of paramount importance. Without the ability to interact effectively with people, success is short-lived. Being able to articulate one's thoughts, purpose, and goals is also a critical skill often needed in situations such as participation in Chambers of Commerce, professional associations, client groups, civic groups, and simple telephone conversations. Failure to develop effective interpersonal skills can be the death knell of a small business.

Organizational skills and attention to detail are essential to operating a small business and require the watchful eye of an effective manager. That is not to say that the owner of a small business should involve him or herself in the minute details of business operations. Rather, it implies that a keen, watchful eye on the daily operation is something that any successful small business owner must maintain.

This logically leads to the next critical skill—*the ability to delegate effectively*. Small business owners must be free to market their enterprise outside the office. This begins with smart advertising to attract high quality employees, screening and interviewing applicants, and hiring qualified personnel. With highly capable personnel, a small business owner positions him/herself to engage in effective marketing of the business. Without these elements in place, delegation of tasks becomes difficult if not impossible. The result is a small business owner who is held hostage by the minutia of management, rather than free to sell his product in the community.

Strange as it may sound, strong *accounting and financial management skills* are not a prerequisite for the successful operation of a small business. A broad knowledge of this area and the ability to identify problems is critical. However, involvement in the daily accounting process is unnecessary and counterproductive. Here again, it's crucial to hire qualified personnel and delegate these tasks. One factor sometimes overlooked by small business owners is the importance of hiring people who possess a strong sense of professional ethics—in other words, someone who can be trusted to manage money. With this in place, once again the small business owner is free to do what is most critical to operational efficiency and effectiveness—marketing.

Writing skills are another important element of managing a business. In today's world of instant messaging, email, and text messaging, a business owner must be able to communicate effectively in writing, whether preparing a cogent memorandum, email message or letter to a prospective client. It is easy to pass this skill off as old-fashioned and out of touch with our cyber age. However, society continues to place a very high premium on the written word.

Personal Characteristics and Values

Personal characteristics that are important to running a small business are somewhat more amorphous and less easily recognizable. Of course, many of these traits are learned through life experience.

Honesty and trustworthiness are essential parts of business ownership. No one wants to conduct business with a dishonest or deceitful individual. This not only applies to money transactions, it also applies to the reliability of one's word in the world of business. A businessperson who develops a reputation for reneging on his or her word will soon find his or her peers very reluctant to work with them. Professional isolation becomes the cross that this person will bear.

Hard work, drive and perseverance are several additional characteristics and core values for a business-person that can make or break a small company. The ability to take the time to assure that all aspects of the business are operating well is critical. An owner who walks away from this responsibility on a regular basis will soon find that the business he or she has worked to build will collapse in short order.

A sense of community is an important, yet often-neglected factor in a business's success. Participation in civic affairs, "giving back to the community," and a sense of commitment to those who are less fortunate are the hallmark of a strong sense of community. This, of course, has benefits to those in need—children, students, the elderly, the poor, the homeless and others—and spin-off unintended benefits to the business owner. Community recognition for service at no profit reaps intangible rewards.

The task of starting one's own business is both challenging and tenuous if an entrepreneur does not go into the venture with his or her eyes wide open. A touch of common sense coupled with some basic skills and a sense of determination is the recipe for success.

The skills necessary to operate a business efficiently and effectively are numerous, some tangible, some intangible. Some skills will never be learned in a classroom, but come from life experience as well as trial and error.

Dr. Ralph G. Perrino

NOTES

About the Author

Dr. Ralph Perrino has been an educator and business owner in the Northern Virginia area for more than 30 years. He has taught sociology, political science, and business management at Northern Virginia Community College since 1984. In that capacity, he has seen many students in his classes who have either come to the community college because they failed in their first attempt at a four-year institution, or because they chose to defer college until after working or military service. Many of the students Dr. Perrino has taught have also been diagnosed with various learning disabilities that present challenges and impediments to the learning process. It was for this reason that Dr. Perrino established Northern Virginia Tutoring Service in 1995. He saw a need to provide practical advice and service to students and families who face the myriad of challenges associated with the education process. Many parents and students have benefited from the time Dr. Perrino has taken for individual consultations.

The field of education is replete with issues that seem complex, confusing and, at times, intractable to many parents and students. The result is that many parents and students often do not know where to find honest, factual information to guide them, or they make decisions without seeking authoritative sources of assistance. Dr. Perrino has long been committed to helping students and parents maneuver through these issues.

Dr. Perrino has always felt that contributing to the welfare of the community is an integral part of business ownership. He has served as both president of the board of Washington Independent Services for Educational Resources (WISER) and chairman of the board of the Greater Falls Church Chamber of Commerce. He is currently on the board of the Fairfax Partnership for Youth, a board member of Friends of David M. Brown Planetarium, Falls Church Education Foundation, Falls Church Public Schools Business in Education Program, and the Arlington County Public Schools Partners in Education Program. Dr. Perrino is a member of the Asian American Chamber of Commerce and a member of the Northern Virginia Black Chamber of Commerce where he serves as chairman of its Scholarship Committee. Dr. Perrino also serves on the boards of Creative Cauldron and Faction of Fools Theater Companies.

Dr. Perrino was honored with a 2009 James B. Hunter III Community Hero Award for his work in support of programs at Patrick Henry Elementary School, where he mentors students from kindergarten through fifth grade. The Arlington School Administrators recognized Dr. Perrino's civic involvement and experience by awarding him the prestigious Arlington School Administrators 2006 Civic Award. He was also awarded the Outstanding Adjunct Faculty Award by Northern Virginia Community College in 2012.

31882064R00126

Made in the USA
Middletown, DE
15 May 2016